SCHOOLHOUSE MEMORIES

HOQUIAM, WASHINGTON

DK TAYLOR

BOOT TOP BOOKS
Lacey, WA

Schoolhouse Memories is a work of nonfiction: letters, articles, family stories, and photographs from various collections and sources.

Copyright© 2024 by Karen Bishop - All Rights Reserved

Library of Congress Cataloging-in-Publication Data

Bishop, Karen (KB Taylor/DK Taylor)

Caress, Diane (DK Taylor)

LCCN: 2024914708
Schoolhouse Memories
Hoquiam, Washington

DK Taylor-1st ed.

p. cm: includes bibliographical references.

Summary: Based on the various collections

ISBN: 9798985655629

1. Hoquiam Schools. 2. Hoquiam, WA history. 3.) Grays Harbor, WA history 4. 1900-1960 Early Americana

Front cover: McKinley School, 1911, First Grade,
Great-aunt Viorene Cline pictured.
(Authors' collection)
McKinley School Insert:
(Courtesy of the Polson Museum, Hoquiam, Wash., 1989.036.0006)

Printed in the United States of America

September 2024

Boot Top Books

Lacey, WA

www.kb-taylor.com

*To Douglas
the keeper of our memories*

AUTHORS' NOTE

Our great-grandmother, Nettie Connell, also referred to as Nettie Connell Taylor, arrived to Hoquiam, Washington in 1896 to teach school. In 1898, she became assistant principal of Hoquiam Public Schools, quite an accomplishment for a woman of that era. We wanted to know more about her and the teaching methods used, which led us to the schools.

Each new piece of fragmented history unraveled the realization that little had been documented in book form and even less about Hoquiam's elementary schools. Diane's extensive research redirected our focus to include all of the schools, which resulted in the creation of this book.

Our Great-uncle, Lester Hanson, sometimes spelled Hansen, was also instrumental in Hoquiam's early school years, but from a student's perspective. Lester entered first grade at McKinley in 1897 and graduated in 1909. He was a member of multiple high-school committees and a participant of all of the sports teams, plus the Athletic Association treasurer, and the manager of basketball. He was also a member and later a president of Hoquiam's first Alumni Association formed in 1911.

Our cousin, Viorene "Gladys" Muhlhauser (née May), was a member of the Grays Harbor Genealogical Society. She attended Emerson Grade School, Hoquiam Junior High, and was a 1940 Hoquiam High School graduate. We inherited her historical collection and many of the artifacts in this book, including some of her school documents, are included.

Authors - DK Taylor

ACKNOWLEDGMENTS

A special thank you to Mr. Larry R. Jones, Assistant Superintendent, Principal, and Teacher of Hoquiam Public Schools for a span of forty years. Mr. Jones' firsthand accounts of the school system, stories, and artifacts fueled this project to life.

To Polson Museum Director John Larson and Secretary Mary Thornton, thank you for lending your hand and permission to use Polson Museum's cataloged pictures.

To Mr. Lee H. Thomasson. Thank you for your first-person stories that encapsulated the post-war years. Your memories and memorabilia brought a personal touch to this book. So grateful to have you aboard.

To Mrs. Mary Lillegard (née Williams), thank you for adding the missing pieces to the Washington School story.

To the Hoquiam Public Library team. Thank you for your assistance. We appreciate your friendly, helpful staff.

CHEHALIS COUNTY RENAMED TO "GRAYS HARBOR COUNTY" IN 1915
(Authors' collection)

FIVE RIVERS: the Chehalis, Hoquiam, Humptulips, Wishkah, and Wynoochee, flow into and form Grays Harbor Bay.

INTRODUCTION

BY THE SUMMER OF 1858, the government engineers had completed their survey and opened entry to the township surrounding the Hoquiam River. Claims could be made by homestead or by cash at $1.25 an acre. The quantity was unlimited.[1] The following year, 1859, paved the course of Hoquiam's future. This was the year that James Karr and Edward Campbell arrived.

JAMES KARR

AFTER SETTLING their father's Indiana estate in 1855, James Karr, hereafter also referred to as Karr, and his brother, Henry, headed west. On their travels through Washington Territory, they met Mr. Goodell[a] of Mound Prairie whose son Ed had been helping with the Grays Harbor survey. Ed told the Karr brothers about the area and of the river called Hoquiam.

August 1859, the brothers hued a canoe and rounded Cow Point[b], landing where the first schoolhouse was afterward built.[2] James Karr then proceeded upland on the south side. Henry chose a site directly across the river from his brother. Both men cleared their land and built their homestead shacks.[3] Later that same year, Scotsmen Edward Campbell with his three brothers claimed land on the north side of the river.[4]

In 1860, Karr, age twenty-six, secured his Hoquiam claim as a preemption, the homestead law had not yet been passed, and established a brickyard at Cosmopolis, making him the first brickmaker of the county. He had learned the brickmaker trade as a youth. This same year, he acted as the secretary of the first political meeting held in Grays Harbor and became one of the first "school teachers" of Chehalis County, teaching at the newly built Cosmopolis school.[5] The Cosmopolis school's fireplace and chimney were built with bricks from Karr's brickyard. Once the school was completed, twelve to fifteen pupils attended. In addition to teaching common academics, Karr introduced the students to music. He had perfected the violin from his travels to Nashville, Illinois and Nevada City, California.[6] The next year, he taught in Montesano,

---

[a] Goodell, also spelled Goddell.
[b] Cow Point was a landmark near the Hoquiam River mouth. At a distance, the spruce root and trunk looked like a large cow.

where he was largely paid in cattle. In the winter of 1862-63, he was the schoolmaster at Mound Prairie. He then traveled to Oregon to see his brother, Henry, who was now working there.

During his Oregon visit, Karr met his future wife, Abbie Walker, a school teacher in Hillsboro. Mr. Goodell of Mound Prairie had given Karr a picture of Miss Walker, with a request to return it to her. After a very short courtship, James Karr and Abbie Walker married on September 14, 1863. They later settled at Karr's Hoquiam River homestead where they lived for the next forty years and raised twelve children.[7]

ON JUNE 4, 1866, the first election held in Chehalis County elected Karr as county auditor.[8] He filled this office for twelve years at no salary. The incumbent following was allowed fees and three dollars per day.[9] During the years of 1875, 1882, and 1893, Mr. Karr was elected as a Republican state legislator. As a member of the legislature, he supported many measures which had far reaching beneficial effects.[10] He was also a Mason and charter member of the Hoquiam lodge of that order, and a director of Hoquiam's first school board.

KARR VALUED EDUCATION and ensured that children were offered opportunities that he never received as a youth. His father died when he was three-years-old. When his mother remarried, the new family moved to Illinois and settled on an eighty-acre tract of raw land. Before title was secured, James' stepfather passed away, which forced another move, putting the Karr family in financial turmoil. His mother later met her third husband, Mr. Storick. He moved the family to a good farm, but required hard labor from the children.[11] When James expressed a desire to attend school, his mother encouraged the idea, but not his new stepfather, so at age fourteen, James left home.

He hired out on a farm for a summer wage of five dollars per month. After proving his worth, he took on additional work at better pay, which he used for books and clothing. That winter, he attended school. The following summer he entered an apprenticeship as a brickmaker, which afforded him the same opportunity of school in the winter. For six years James continued this process: working the summers and attending school in the winters. He was also mentored by one of his teachers, John Leeper, a graduate of McKendree College of Illinois. Approaching nineteen, Karr with a business partner established and operated a brickyard, which enabled him to pay his board and devote an entire year to study. During this period, he acquired a knowledge of algebra, natural philosophy, and astronomy. He then taught school for a term, then moved to the study of medicine and worked as a clerk in a drug store.

HOQUIAM'S FIRST SCHOOL was in the abandoned split-cedar cabin of Johnny James, the second one he had built and upstream from the first at the mouth of the Hoquiam River. In 1864, Sidney Dunlap had settled in East Hoquiam and joined the others to form a school board. However, five children were necessary to establish a school, and it was not until 1873 that five were of available age: three Karr children and two Campbell. School was officially started in either 1873 or 1874[c] and the term lasted three months. Julia Andrew was their first teacher.[12] (Also listed by other sources as Mr. Julius Andrews.)

The Karr's provided educational opportunities for all of their children. During the summer months, the children attended the Hoquiam Public School, and when the term was over, the big family bedroom was converted into a schoolroom with homemade desks. The parents were the instructors, until the older sisters assumed the task of teaching. Mr. Karr believed firmly that girls should be given the same chance as boys. According to his daughters, they received the same educational advantages as their brothers.

Three of his daughters graduated from the University of Washington and daughter, Ruth, now Mrs. McKee, had a Master of Arts degree and was a member of Phi Beta Kappa. Her admission was gained only by a high scholarship.[13] That winter a parliamentary law club was formed—the first on the Harbor—and Mr. Karr acted as president. His children received training there, which was proven valuable in later years.[14]

By 1861 most of the land along the lower Hoquiam had been taken. The claims of James Karr, Ed Campbell, and Johnny James were incorporated into the city of Hoquiam.[15] James Karr, a member of the school board, sold several lots to the school district for the new McKinley School. "A splendid edifice and the absolute pride and joy of the town," he said. He later sold lots for the Lincoln School too. Karr Avenue was named in his honor and to mark his place in Grays Harbor's history.

---

[c]School start year was either 1873 or 1874. One source claimed 1873. *The River Pioneers*, Pg 372, author: E. Van Syckle stated J. James house was fitted out for a school in 1874.

EDWARD CAMPBELL

EDWARD CAMPBELL worked as a printer's devil[d] in Ohio for three years at $10 a year with room and board. He had bigger dreams, so caught a riverboat to Missouri, then hired on as a herdsman for a 150-head cattle drive to California. There he dug gold for three years. When he heard about the opportunities in the Pacific Northwest, twenty-four-year-old Edward Campbell with his three brothers, sailed to Portland, traveled overland to Olympia, and on to Hoquiam, landing at Cow Point by canoe in 1859, shortly after Karr.[16]

CAMPBELL CLAIMED land on the north side of the river to the Aberdeen line.[17] Both Karr and Campbell went into the cattle business, prospering with beef and butter. Campbell expanded with hogs for ham and bacon.[18]

The year 1867 was a significant one for Ed Campbell as well as for the new settlement of Hoquiam. In January, he married Harriet Boyce (née Scammon) of Montesano. This same year he applied for a post office. With the application, Campbell had to name the settlement. At that time only the river used the name Hoquiam and the settlers used various spellings. The most common, Hoxium. After conferring with brothers, William and Johnny James, they, along with Campbell, decided that the settlement should be named after the river, but needed a better spelling and settled on Hoquiam. Once the application was approved, a small split-cedar shed was erected on the Hoquiam River bank to serve as the post office. Campbell was appointed postmaster and held the position for the next twenty years until his retirement in 1887.

As the postmaster, Campbell and his family modified their lives to the constant arrivals and departures of locals and strangers. Their location became an accessible stop for travelers who expected to be fed and housed, which resulted with the Campbells opening a boardinghouse. At times they housed as many as sixty guests, many forced to sleep in the barn at fifty cents a head [19] Mrs. Campbell was also known for her excellent cooking, which attracted travelers to come off-course for one of her meals.

Later, Campbell purchased one of the disbanded Fort Chehalis houses. As it was disassembled, he numbered each piece of lumber and rebuilt it on his

---

[d] Printer's devil: a younger boy or man working below the level of a printing-house apprentice.

Riverside Avenue and Eighteenth Street lot. It became the family home where he and his wife raised their six children. Two of their daughters, Laura and Rose Agnes, attended the first school.

Campbell also held the office of deputy auditor and the justice of the peace for fourteen years. Both of the Campbell sons went on to higher education and returned to Hoquiam to work. Horace, who graduated from the College of Physicians and Surgeons of Columbia College in New York, practiced in Hoquiam until his death on February 2, 1907, at the age of thirty-five. William, a graduate of the Harvard Law School, served many years as a Grays Harbor County superior court judge.[20]

THE JAMES FAMILY

IN 1857, SAMUEL JAMES of Mound Prairie with his sons Samuel, William and Johnny rowed to Grays Harbor in a big war canoe. William and the two Samuels claimed 200 acres eastward of the Humptulips' river mouth, behind the sentinel rock later named James Rock, and built a split-cedar log house. They also grafted apple shoots onto wild crabapple to start an orchard. Johnny James (AKA: John R. James), N.E. Goodell, and Levi Gates built their rustic log cabins at the mouth of the Hoquiam River.[21] Johnny James afterward built a sturdier second cabin upriver, which later became the town's community center and Hoquiam's first school.

In 1866, Johnny James married Mary Scammon, sister to Ed Campbell's wife. After proving up his claims, Johnny moved his family back to Mound Prairie where the James' clan had previously established a large family colony.[22]

GEORGE H. EMERSON

ANOTHER MILESTONE that changed Hoquiam, was the arrival of George H. Emerson in 1880. Emerson, an agent for lumber baron Asa M. Simpson of San Francisco, arrived from California to scout for timber and a mill site for the coast. He had first decided on Cosmopolis for the site, but the owner was wavering on the price, so Emerson ventured down to Hoquiam to talk to James Karr and Ed Campbell.

After a productive meeting and a sampling of Mrs. Campbell's famous blackberry pie, Emerson determined that Hoquiam was the place. He purchased 300 acres of land, including a riverside site for the sawmill from Johnny James, and returned the following year on the little brig *Orient* loaded with machinery for the new Northwestern Lumber Company. [23] The mill attracted businesses and settlers, and by 1885, the town was platted with a permanent population of two to three hundred residents. [24]

A year before incorporation, Hoquiam's new "city fathers:" George Emerson, John F. Soule, and North Western Mill Company secretary, stockholder, and boss logger W.D. Mack, lobbied for legislation favorable to the lumber industry and for the Northern Pacific Railroad to extend its line to Hoquiam. Their publicized trips to metropolitan areas resulted in a flood of financial speculators and immigrants to work in the mills and the woods. Hoquiam's population tripled from 400 to 1,500 as did the expansion of the city and property values. [25] On May 21, 1890, Hoquiam was incorporated as a city. Its first city council was: John Richardson, George W. France, O.M. Murphy, and Peter Autzen. J.T. Burns served as the first mayor. [26]

HOQUIAM, WASHINGTON 1884
Edward Campbell home (foreground left)
Johnny James' split-cedar cabin, used for the first school,
was across the river to the far right along the riverbank.
(Courtesy of the Polson Museum, Hoquiam, Wash, 1986.079.0046)

HOQUIAM FERRY
(Courtesy of the Polson Museum, Hoquiam, Wash., 1986.051.0002)

BEFORE THE BRIDGES were erected, the only transport across the river was by boat. It is believed that the children on the north, the east, and the south side of the river used the ferry as their river transport to and from school.

In this picture, the ferry is landing within walking distance to Hoquiam's first schoolhouse, which was Johnny James' second cabin. It was located where the Hoquiam Sash and Door Company later stood at Fifth and H Street, just beyond the west approach of the Hoquiam Riverside Bridge.

CHAPTER 1
HOQUIAM'S FIRST SCHOOLS

FIVE PUPILS WERE NECESSARY to establish a school, and it was not until 1873 that five were of available age: Olive (7), Beatrice (6) and Elk (4) Karr plus Rose Agnes (9) and Laura (4) Campbell. Hoquiam's first school was in the abandoned cabin of Johnny James, the second one he had built and upstream from the first, near the present Fifth and H Streets.

School was retrofitted in 1873 and officially opened by 1874.[1] The school term lasted three months. Julius Andrews was one of the first teachers[2] and was paid $20 a month.

BELIEVED TO BE HOQUIAM'S FIRST SCHOOL
(Courtesy of the Polson Museum, Hoquiam, Wash., 2011.065.0188)

Polson Museum documentation, 2011.065.0188, states that this picture is believed to be Johnny James' second cabin that was used for Hoquiam's first school. This is based on the archives: *Reminiscences of John R. James* [e]; Chapter: Cabin at Hoquiam; archived in JBL's Hoquiam Pioneer People file.

Excerpts:

---

[e] Johnny James, AKA: John R. James.

"Hiving [sic][f] filed on 160 acres of land at Hoquiam I first built a very poor cabin near the mouth of the river where the North Western mill stands. I made the cabin out of alder logs, a very crude affair. Slashed the willows and alders and brush for an acre around the cabin. **Afterwards I built a cabin out of lumber, about 60 rods south of Mr. Karr's E. and W. line on the bank of the river."**

"We used to build temporary crafts for freighting supplies to the Harbor. Would get a gunwale of 2 or 3 inch plank 24 feet long and about 30 inches wide, nail (spike) the bottom boards on; put in a false bottom, load it down and control it on the river by use of a big oar (sweeps) at each end; drift with the current; generally make these trips when the river was at good stage; often drift from Grand Mound to Montesano in one day; that is, by late traveling—rather risky traveling after dark, never above tide water—the shadows from the trees make objects very indistinct after dark on the water—not safe to navigate after dark on a rapid river. After unloading we would break up the craft. **In this way I got most of the lumber for the first mansion on the west bank of the Hoquiam. My niece, Miss Laura Campbell, gave a very good description of my homestead house when it was used for school purposes after I went to Grand Mound to live."**

"Mr. Karr built a stone fireplace in the north wall, using the rock from the bluff on the other side of the river where there was a spring; built the fireplace too high up to the arch for such a small cabin; looked like about as much fireplace as cabin."

KARR'S EAST TO WEST line on the bank of the river, that John James refers to above, is believed to be Emerson Avenue. Emerson is several blocks from the location of the first school, which John James states is about 60 rods south of Karr's E. and W. line.

SIX YEARS of a leaky roof and tides reaching the doorstop of John James' old cabin, necessitated the building of a new school upriver where it served as the school for the next two years. Hereafter, also referred to as School #2. It was the later site of the E.K. Wood Sawmill. During this period, another school was placed in the store of the Northwestern Lumber Company.[3] It is assumed that the NW Lumber Company school was for the mill-workers' children only and

---

[f] [Sic], Latin: *sic erat scriptum* (thus was it written), quoted exactly as originally written.

not part of the Hoquiam school district. It is also unknown how long it was in operation.

In the early years, Hoquiam along with all of the area west of Cosmopolis belonged to School District No. 5.[4] This included Aberdeen. In the case of Aberdeen's one-room schoolhouse on Market Street, their pupils furnished their own benches.[5]

Hoquiam's early school roster:[6]

1873-74: Directors: James A. Karr, Samuel Benn, Edward Campbell.
Clerk: Edward Campbell. Teacher: Clara Nye.
1874-75: Same directors and clerk. Teacher: Julius Andrews.[9]
1875-77: Same directors and clerk. Teacher: Fannie Baldwin.
1877-78: Same directors.
Clerk: Samuel Benn. Teacher: Mrs. M.B. Virgil.
1878-79: Same directors and clerk. Teacher: Cornelia Newton.
1879-80: Same directors.
Clerk: H.H. Halbert. Teacher: Cornelia Newton.
1880-81: Directors: Edward Campbell, Samuel Benn, H.H. Halbert.
Clerk: H.H. Halbert. Teacher: Mrs. M.B. Virgil.
1881-82: Directors: Edward Campbell, John R. Walker, H.H Halbert
Clerk: H.H. Halbert. Teacher: W.S. McCready.

IN 1882, THE STEVENS SCHOOL, named after Territorial Governor Isaac Stevens, was built at Ninth and I Streets, hereafter also referred to as School #3. By 1884, Hoquiam had grown in territory and pupils and qualified as its own school district, forming District No. 28. This was also the same year that Samuel Benn's name disappeared off of the 1884-1885 Hoquiam roster.

Serving as Hoquiam's only public school, all grades one through eight were taught at Stevens. The first and second floors were a one-room schoolhouse concept. The first floor more than likely encompassed grades one through four and the second floor, grades five through eight. It is assumed that the pupils sat at tables lined with benches and later replaced with desks and chairs.

Note: The first school board was formed in 1864, but they had to wait until 1873 when five children reached the available age to establish a school, and was officially opened by 1874.

STEVENS SCHOOL
Ninth and I Street, Hoquiam, WA
(Courtesy of Larry R. Jones' collection)

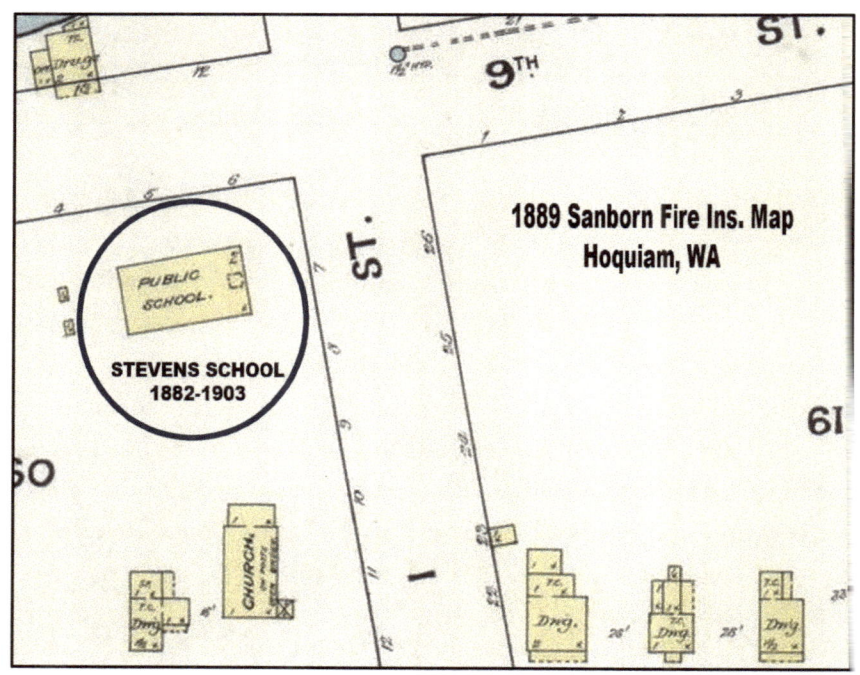

STEVENS SCHOOL (Ninth and "I")
"I" Street was later renamed Simpson Avenue
1889 SANBORN FIRE INSURANCE MAP, HOQUIAM, WA
(Library of Congress, public domain)

After Hoquiam's population had tripled in 1889, Stevens was partially enlarged, turning it into a six or eight-room building,[7] and had a headcount of approximately twenty-five pupils.[8] The next year, a two-year-course system was put into action by Principal W.L. Adams for Hoquiam's first high school.[9] With the completion of McKinley School in 1892, all classes except for sixth-grade were transferred. Sixth grade remained at Stevens for another ten years or so.

Hoquiam's school roster after the completion of Stevens School:

1883-84: Directors: John R. Walker, Samuel Benn, H.H. Halbert. Clerk: H.H. Halbert. Teacher: Ella Benjamin.
1884-85: Directors: Edward Campbell, George H. Emerson, H.H. Halbert. Clerk: H.H. Halbert. Teacher: Mary White
1885-86: Directors: Edward Campbell, George H. Emerson, A.H. Holman. No clerk. Teacher: A.W. Hutchins.
1886-87: Same directors and clerk. Teacher: Ada Sprague.
1887-88: Directors: George H. Emerson, James A. Karr, E.T. Balch. Clerk: Peter Autzen, Jessie Murch (resigned). Teacher: Ola Gillespie.
1888-89: Same directors and clerk. Teacher-principal: J.D. Dean.
1889-90: Directors: George H. Emerson, O.M Moore, Edward Campbell. O.M Murphy appointed; Peter Autzen resigned as clerk. George E. Watson appointed; J.D. Dean reassigned as teacher. W.L. Adams appointed.

STEVENS SCHOOL 1897 (NINTH AND I Streets)
Teacher: Milton Richardson, Sixth-grade class
(Courtesy of the Polson Museum, Hoquiam, Wash. 1986.051.0004)

In 1891, planning for another school was in the make. This new school was later named McKinley, after our 25th President, William McKinley, who was elected on November 4, 1896.

Hoquiam March 28th, 1891
Regular Meeting Board Trustees of School District No. 28
Members present: Geo H. Emerson, J.A. Karr and Seth Warren

Records of previous meeting read and approved. The secondary reported the payment of sundry bills. On motion, action of Secretary was approved.

Motion by J. A. Karr that it is the sense of this Board that a building site for [sic] school building be secured in Karr's River addition and over in vicinity of 5th and L Streets, Hoquiam. (Motion carried.) On motion, the present session of Schools shall terminate on May 22, 1891. So ordered.

Motion by Warren that School Clerk be instructed to have school tab graded sufficient for comfort. (Carried.)

Motion by J. A. Karr that the course of study presented by Wm Adams, principal, be adopted and spread upon the records. (Carried.) (Hoquiam March 28th, 1891, Regular Meeting Board Trustees of Schools, district No 28).

Prior to the opening of the new school, Principal W.L. Adams outlined a "Graded School-Course-of-Study" for each grade, one through eight, by the respective departments. First grade, the "Primary Department," specified pencils and crayons, plus instruction on hygiene with special attention to sitting and standing positions. Second and third graders, the "Secondary Department," springboarded off of the first-grade fundamentals, except third grade added arithmetic, writing, and geography. Fourth and fifth graders, the "Intermediate Department," were learning the names of the United States and their capitals plus how to spell them.[10]

Sixth and seventh grade classes, the "Principal's Department," were developing their writing skills: notes, drafts, receipts, bills, and letters. In Eighth grade, algebra, civil government, and English literature was also introduced.

Prior to 1891, school ended after the eighth grade. With the creation of a new course study plan for higher studies, ninth and tenth grades, Hoquiam's first high school students would be graduating in 1892. All grades, excluding first and second, had identical school terms: fall was sixteen weeks and spring, twenty. Below is the "Course of Study" for first graders prepared by Principal/Superintendent Adams in 1891. Original copies for all grades can be viewed at the back of this book.

HOQUIAM GRADED SCHOOL
PRIMARY DEPARTMENT COURSE OF STUDY

Reader: Chart and First Reader, completed with drill in reading script characters.

Numbers: Teach numbers one to ten. Follow the course outlined in Parker's Talks on Teaching. Chapters XVI and XVII. (Wentworth's Primary in the hands of teacher.)

Language: Teach the correct use of language by constantly correcting common errors. Give special attention to terminal marks and capitals.

Writing: Use only pencils and crayons. Teach correct forms of small letters and capitals.

Spelling: Teach both oral and written from reading lessons. Attention to sounds of letters.

Hygiene: Occasional short lectures on laws of health. Special attention to correct positions in sitting and standing.

Drawing: Daily drill in simple exerciser. (Hull's Exercises in the hands of teacher.)

On June 3, 1892, the first Hoquiam High School graduation from Stevens held a special ceremony at the Hoquiam Theater. Those first graduates were: Hearst Ansley, Thayer Lamb, Addie France (née Rowland), and Edith Peel (née Tuttle). Over the next decade and a half, graduating class size remained at single-digit.

**MCKINLEY SCHOOL (School #4) 1892
HOQUIAM, WASHINGTON**
(Courtesy of the Polson Museum, Hoquiam, Wash, 1989.036.0006)

IN THE FALL OF 1892, the new school, later named McKinley, was completed. "A splendid edifice and the absolute pride and joy of the town," said James Karr of the new school located at Emerson and Hayes Avenues. The land had been previously owned by Karr, who sold two lots from his addition for $2,000 to the school district in 1891. The school building itself cost $10,980.

TALL SPRUCE TREES BEHIND the schoolhouse extended to the hill and all along the west.[11] Many of Hoquiam's streets had already been named.

Streets running north and west, including Emerson Avenue, were named after famous pioneers, such as George Emerson and James Karr. Their cross streets were named after U.S. Presidents: Garfield, Grant, and Hayes, listing three.

Lettered street names, starting with H, were used on the south side of Emerson Avenue and intersected with numbered cross-streets like: First, Second, and Third. Many of these alphabet and numbered streets also connected to Emerson Avenue at separate angles.

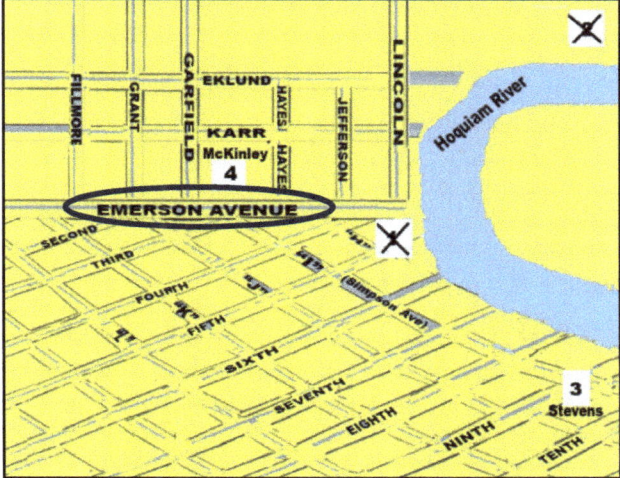

1892 MAP OF HOQUIAM SCHOOLS
(Authors' collection)

Various-sized sloughs snaked through Hoquiam which caused havoc to the children, forcing them to keep a watchful eye for the tide so they wouldn't show up to school with wet muddy feet. To remedy some of this, the walkways from H to K Streets were built of planks sitting in the air that extended all the way to Emerson Avenue. [12]

Excerpt, *School Days' 1900*, Clara Knack Dooley, page 34:

"I remember the hollow sound in walking on bridges downtown when you could not see the slough. On a fine rainy day, where there were flood tides, the frogs had a wonderful time. I judged by their croaking that they did, for I never saw them."

HOQUIAM'S RAISED WALKWAYS OVER SLOUGHS
(Courtesy of the Polson Museum, Hoquiam, Wash, 1977.073.0001)

THE BRUCE AND LAMB Drug Store carried all of the new books and school supplies. On the first day of school and days before, children with their parents flocked to the store. Lining the shelves were new books, pencils, pens and erasers, and tablets of all sizes with pictured covers, plus wooden pencil boxes with its own lock and key. To carry the key, students would drape a tied ribbon around their necks. For the first few weeks, the teachers had to listen to the opening and closing of those noisy boxes, all in unison.[13]

Each new school year started in September. At the new school, first, second, and third-grade classes were all located on the first floor, above the basement level. The first-grade class was to the left of the front door. Second grade was directly across the hall and the third graders were taught in the rear classroom, next to the stairway ascending to the upper floors.

The second and third floors had a bump-out at the front, which allowed for extra classrooms. The fourth, fifth, seventh, and eighth graders occupied the second story and the two-year high school classes were held on the very top third floor. Sixth grade was still taught at the old Stevens School, where it remained through the next decade.[14] The school, now with an outlined structure, provided final grade-standing cards, plus a Certificate of Promotion to the next grade. Before the school was renamed McKinley in 1897, it was referred to as Hoquiam Public Schools.[h]

**1895 CERTIFICATE of PROMOTION
From FOURTH to FIFTH Grade**
(Authors' collection)

---

[d] Belle Cline (née Rodgers), authors' great-grandmother.

HOQUIAM'S FIRST SCHOOLS

**1895-1896 "BELLE RODGERS"
FINAL STANDINGS CARD**
(Authors' collection)

**1897 HIGH SCHOOL GRADUATING CLASS
MCKINLEY SCHOOL (Ninth and Tenth Grades only)**
Second row, far right: **Superintendent Prof. Chamberlain**.
Girls: Ollie Dunning, Addie Hull, Laura Reed, Daisy Spicer, Ruth Townsend, Jeannie Wheeler. **(Female teacher unknown, center back row.)**
Boys: A.C. Girard, Oliver Morris, Thomas Spencer
(Courtesy of the Polson Museum, Hoquiam, Wash., 1997.081.0004)

CLARA KNACK, AGE SEVEN, and her older siblings started at McKinley in 1899. Her book paints a vivid picture of Hoquiam and McKinley School during this period. She listed Miss Howes as her teacher when she entered the second grade, noting that the children read from the "Franklin Second Reader" and that they were separated into divisions. The "A" Division held the more-advanced, brighter students of each class. Many times these students were advanced to the next level, such as from second to third grade. Size, not age, was sometimes used as a factor for grouping grade level as well.

The 1899 faculty included: Miss Dutcher, first grade; Miss Howes (later Mrs. Kuhn), second grade; Miss Kellogg, third grade; fourth-grade teacher, unknown; Mr. Philbrick, fifth grade; Miss Connell [i] (later Mrs. Taylor), seventh and eighth grades; and Principal/Superintendent Williams, high-school classes. Mr. Richardson taught sixth grade at the old Stevens' school.

> Excerpts, *School Days' 1900*, Clara Knack Dooley, pages 25-28:
>
> *"Mr. P.A. Williams was the superintendent of the schools, and Mrs. Howes (she later became Mrs. Kuhn) was our teacher. Miss Dorothy Dutcher was the first-grade teacher in the room across the hall from us. Miss Abigail Kellogg was the third-grade teacher in the rear room.*
>
> *Upstairs there was the fourth grade and I don't remember the teacher's name. Mr. Edward Philbrick had the fifth grade, and Mrs. Nettie Taylor (or perhaps she was Miss Connell then?) had the seventh and eighth grades. The two-year high school was taught by Mr. Williams. Sixth grade was taught by Milton Richardson on the first floor of the old schoolhouse on Ninth and I Street."* (Stevens School)

At the opening of the new school (McKinley) in 1892, William Adams remained as the principal, superintendent, and the instructor of Hoquiam's first high school, grades nine and ten. By school term, September 1893, Adams was replaced by A.G. Cushman, who remained until 1895. It is unknown if Adams remained as the high-school instructor, but it appeared that superintendents weren't a life-long career. Between the school terms 1895 and 1901, two more superintendents had come and gone: F.J. Chamberlain 1895 through 1898. P.A. Williams 1898 through 1901.

---

[i] Nettie Connell Taylor, authors' great-grandmother.

WHEN DR. A.D. WARDE[j] arrived in 1901, he was elected principal and superintendent plus the high-school instructor. He also added a third year to the high-school courses.[15] It appeared that he had won the position by impressing new ideas to the powers who had hired him. Dr. Warde, which he insisted to be called, imparted a different style that intimidated many of the students and maybe some of the teachers. Most of the small kids were afraid of him. He would come into a room unannounced and pick a pupil to humiliate. His reasons were unknown, but it could be as simple as the student wearing patches on their clothes.[16]

Excerpts, *School Days' 1900,* Clara Knack Dooley, page 40, Dr. Ward:

"No one, I am sure, going to school in Hoquiam at that time, will ever forget him. The big girls were in the way and his whole attention was on the big boys. And he chose some of the meanest of them to be special pets.

HOQUIAM HIGH SCHOOL CADETS, 1901
(Courtesy of the Polson Museum, Hoquiam, Wash, 2006.058.0139)

L to R (back): Clarence Reuter, Jerry McGillicuddy Jr.
L to R (seated): Clarence Shaw, Chris Reidel, and Fred Smith

He must have thought he was managing a private school for boys, for **he formed a class of cadets***, had the boys get uniforms, and spent much time drilling them. Some boys dropped out of school because their parents refused to buy them uniforms. Dr. Ward was their instructor as well as being the single high-school teacher. How the few freshmen and sophomores learned all of their algebra, geometry, English I and II, their ancient and medieval history, their two years of science, their typing and bookkeeping, I will never know..."*

[j] Dr Warde, in other documentation spelled "Ward."

HIGH-SCHOOL STUDENTS (1901)
Cadets pictured in front and back rows
Dr. Warde (back row, center)
(Courtesy of Polson Museum, Hoquiam, Wash, 2006.058.0149)

THE HIGH-SCHOOL group picture with the cadets (above) encompassed students who would be graduating in 1901 through 1906. During this time, they were being taught at McKinley. At the end of the next school year, 1902, Dr. Warde disappeared as did the cadet uniforms. It can be assumed that school returned to a normal posture, at least for the poor students who feared coming under Dr. Warde's wrath.

<u>Class 1901:</u> Florence Arthaud (née Acteson), Jessie Campbell (née Lycan), Arthur Karr, Hubbard Tuttle, Bertha Wilson (née Brown).

<u>Class 1902:</u> Elene Bailey, Ella Hansen (née Ellingson), Marguerite Harris, Aurilla Isaacson (née Baker), Nellie Sherwood (née Mills), Fred A. Smith.

<u>Class 1903:</u> Jerry McGillicuddy, Chris Reidel, Clarence Reuter.

<u>Class 1904:</u> Susie Lenfesty, Henry Knack, Phoebe Parker, Annabel Walker (née Richardson).

<u>Class 1905:</u> None.

<u>Class 1906:</u> Olga (Ola) Hall, Arthur Winkleman, Ida Whalen (née Annis), Kate Tracy (née Knack).

CENTRAL SCHOOL No. 1 (1903)
(Courtesy of the Polson Museum, Hoquiam, Wash, 2001.018.0121)

IN THE SUMMER OF 1903, Central School (No. 1) was built near the end of I Street (later renamed Simpson Avenue) with the second floor planned for the high school. This same year a fourth year of high school, twelfth grade, under Professor Burkhead's administration, was added. The class of 1906 was the first to complete the full four years of high school.[17] With the addition of this new school and the transfer of seventh and eighth grade to it, the sixth graders were finally reunited with the rest of the student body and placed at McKinley. Stevens School was then used for alternate purposes. In 1904 through 1905, there was an eighth-grade class taught at Stevens, but these students never went on to high school.[18]

The first floor of Central held seventh and eighth-grade classes.

Seventh grade was the first to occupy the only finished room. Most of the second floor and the two basement classrooms were designated for the high school, grades nine through twelve.[19]

**CENTRAL SCHOOL NO. 1
SEVENTH GRADE CLASS**
(Authors' collection)

**HOQUIAM HIGH SCHOOL
CENTRAL NO. 1
(Circa 1904)
"WOODSHOP"
Also referred to as "Manual Training"**
(Courtesy of the Polson Museum, Hoquiam, Wash., 2001.018.0123)

SINCE DR. WARDE'S DEPARTURE, things at the school appeared to be running on an even keel, until midterm 1904 when an incident under the rein of Superintendent H.A. Davee (1903-1904) occurred. E.H. Anderson had filled the superintendent spot the prior year (1902-1903).

EACH YEAR, THE STATE school board established Course of Study programs by grade level, which included optional studies. These were not to be converted; doing so would be a violation of school-policy law. For reasons unknown, tenth-grade optional courses, botany or zoology, had been substituted with the eleventh-grade optional course, physics, at Hoquiam High School during the school term of 1903-1904. All was fine until teacher Mr. Scholl, resigned midterm, then it erupted into a school-board scandal.

Mr. Scholl's replacement, Mr. Buck, immediately dropped the physics class and replaced it with the tenth-grade optional course, botany. He then ordered his pupils to get new text books. Ten of these students objected to the change, stating it'd be detrimental to the year's work. The ten classmates were a mixture of grade levels, most of them sophomores, and petitioned the professor to substitute botany with algebra or arithmetic, which they felt would benefit them in daily life. The petition was signed by: Olga Hall, Ida Annis, Mable Whitney, James Peters, Leal Stevenson, Bessie Dawes, Susie Lenfesty, Henry Knack, Arthur Winkleman, and Annabel Richardson. The petition was declined and the tenth-grade pupils were expelled; it is believed for being too outspoken.

A meeting of the school board was held with some of the parents present to protest against the change. After the board revealed that the new teacher was not equipped to teach physics, a heated discussion broke out. "Courses shouldn't be changed to suit the capacity of teachers," one parent said. Another parent interjected that they had on "good authority" that none of the Hoquiam High School teachers carried a first-grade certificate. There was also talk that the board might be forced to pay out money because the state course was not followed. After this meeting, the dismissed students, Olga (Ola) Hall, Bessie Dawes, and Ida Annis, appealed to the County Superintendent Williams to be reinstated in school.

At the appeal meeting, Morgan and Brewer represented the school board and W.T. Arnold, the tenth-grade pupils. It was revealed that County Superintendent Williams told a Mr. Stevens before the investigation that he'd more than likely side in favor of the school board for policy's sake. As a result, the three students lost their case and were forced to transfer to Aberdeen High School.[20] It is believed that some of the other students who had signed the original petition may have dropped out of school as they do not appear on the 1904, 1906, or 1907 graduating roster. Note: there were no graduates in 1905.

Olga and Ida were later reinstated at Hoquiam. It is unknown what happened to Bessie. But these two students were part of the Class of 1906, which was a major milestone for the Hoquiam Public Schools. This class was the first to complete all four years of high school. They had started first grade at McKinley in 1894, and with the completion of Central No. 1 in 1903, they transferred in their sophomore year to the new school.

Class 1906: Olga Hall, Arthur Winkleman, Ida Whalen (née Annis), Kate Tracy (née Knack).

ON MAY 14, 1904, the *Hoquiam Sawyer* printed an article about another incident. Considerable trouble had arisen at Hoquiam High School between the parents and the teachers, which had resorted in corporal punishment or expulsion. Most of the trouble pointed to a child who had been a "willful transgressor" against school discipline from his teacher. The article stated that interference of parents in these matters, unless there be absolute brutality in the punishment of a child, is harmful, not only to the individual scholar, but the child whose cause is championed by a foolish and shortsighted parent, when an ugly tempered, ill-bred boy should be compelled to respect. [21] It is unknown if the pupil mentioned above was part of the seventh-grade problem occurring at the new school this same year.

At the new school (Central No. 1), a handful of seventh-grade boys had become so unruly that Miss Walker stepped down and taught a lower class to finish out the school year. Next, was Mr. Clark, who was young and tried his best, but he quit before the term was over. When E.L. McDonnell, a Stanford University graduate, arrived, he summed up the situation and got rid of the bad apples in quick order.[22] But Henry A. Davee, Superintendent of Hoquiam Schools, ended his one-year career on May 25, 1904.

Not all was bad that year, the new four-year high school was becoming sports enthused, but not only for the boys. The girls formed their own basketball team.

Class 1907: Leal Adams (née Stevenson), John Carlson, Ruby Dahlstrom (née Annis), Ada Sonnemann (née Pettit), John Richardson, Hazel Tuttle (née Tofflemire.)

Class 1908: Clarence Anderson, Elsie Carr, Betty Chabot, Charles Jacka, Myrtle Lenfesty, Mabelle Mills, Deborah Price (née Carr).

1908 GRADUATING CLASS
(Courtesy of the Polson Museum Hoquiam, Wash.,2000.089.0078)

IN **1908-1909**, HOQUIAM HIGH SCHOOL was at the top of their game in athletics, leading all the other schools in Southwest Washington, but many schools refused to play them, admitting they feared that they would lose.

HOQUIAM BASKETBALL TEAM
1908-1909
Lester Hanson, front holding ball
(Authors' collection)

1908-1909
HOQUIAM BASEBALL TEAM
Lester Hanson, front right, holding glove,
Ernest Bemis, middle right, holding glove
(Courtesy of the Polson Museum, Hoquiam, Wash. 2019.054.0012)

The picture forms an "H"
➡

HOQUIAM FOOTBALL SQUAD
1908-1909
Lester Hanson, sideways, front left
(Authors' collection)

Every member of their graduating class participated in school activities, including the senior class play: "Here's to the Health of Capt. Jinks."

Clara Knack, the 1909 valedictorian, credited the class unity to several teachers. One was E.B Beaty, Principal of both McKinley and Central No. 1, who also taught high-school mathematics, science, algebra, and geometry. He held the school together and was deeply missed when he transferred their junior year to teach at the state college in Corvallis. E.L. McDonnell returned as principal their senior year and taught their class U.S. History. Clara Knack stated, "He stayed with us until we were graduated, and I think we all felt a special fondness for E.L. McDonnell." (*School Days', Pg 56-57*)

Class 1909: Mamie Allen, Roy Boyer, Lee Carlton, Tessie Gillett (née Quaife), Lester Hanson[k], Ruth Hitchings, Clara Dooley (née Knack), Loretta Lewis (née Adelsperger), Frieda McIntosh (née Knack), Albert Pettitt, Austin Steeples.

Faculty: W.T. Walton, superintendent; E.L. McDonnell, principal and history teacher; L. Faye Allen, language, Chester Giblin, mathematics; Nellie Ames, science, Beryl Flood, English and domestic science; William Greenleaf, manual training; W.R. Witham, commercial, and Jane B. Warren, music.

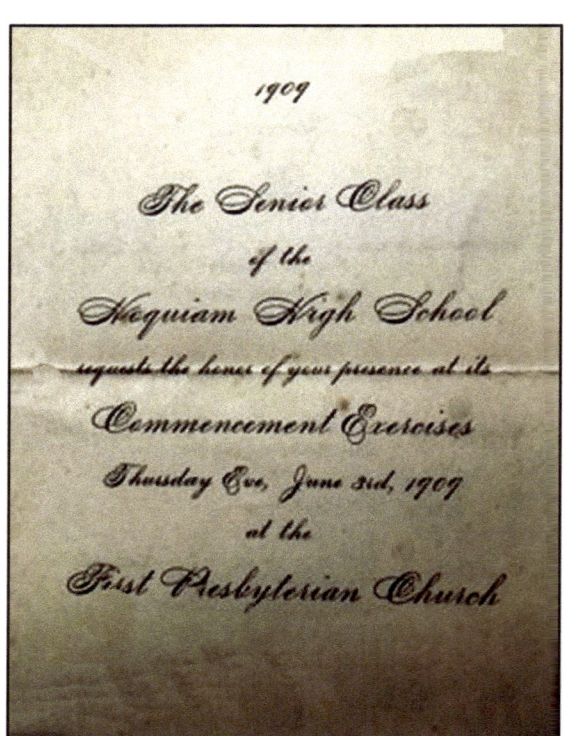

1909 GRADUATION ANNOUNCEMENT
(Authors' collection)

---

[k] Lester Hanson, authors' great-uncle.

THE GRADUATING CLASS of 1910 was the largest of Hoquiam High School so far. Eighteen total and evenly divided, nine boys and nine girls.

Class 1910: Arvid Anderson, Earnest Bemis, Chester Dean, Arthur Eklund, Ernest Eklund, Georgia France, Winifred Hardy, Dora Hitchings, Russell Hoover, Berdeli Hunley, Odessa Hunley, Pearl Marrs (née Holmes), Lottie Ingram, Don Kellogg, March McGlauflin, Ethel Mourant, Ruth Penepacker, Carl Ramstad.

AS THE COMMUNITY GREW to the north, Superintendent Walton and several board members saw the need for another elementary school. They put it on the ballot and got it passed. Built in 1907, Lincoln Elementary accepted its first students in September 1908. The same came true with the opening of Washington School in 1908 for the children across the river.

A—WASHINGTON SCHOOL (1908)

B—LINCOLN ELEMENTARY (BUILT 1907, OPENED 1908)

C—MCKINLEY (1892) CENTRAL NO. 1 (1903)

**FOUR PUBLIC SCHOOLS
1910 ORIGINAL POSTCARD**
(Courtesy of the Polson Museum, Hoquiam, Wash., 2021.23.0253)

CHAPTER 2
TEACHERS OF THE
EARLY SCHOOLS

MR. JULIUS ANDREWS (also listed by other sources as Julia Andrew or Mrs. Julius Andrews[1]) was documented as the first or one of the first school teachers who taught at the abandoned cabin of Johnny James, the second one James had built along the Hoquiam River. The Hoquiam School Roster, lists Clara Nye as the first teacher in 1873-74. Julia Andrew[2] is listed for the next year. The school term lasted three months and the teacher was paid $60 for one term.

JULIUS ANDREWS
(Courtesy of the Polson Museum, Hoquiam, Wash. 2001.031.0003)

On December 24, 1874, Hoquiam celebrated its first community Christmas Eve party at the schoolhouse that lasted until midnight when Mr. Andrews, dressed as Santa, passed out the gifts. Mrs. Karr and Mrs. Campbell with their children were all in attendance. It was reported in the newspaper that all, including Santa, made it home safely.[3]

MR. JULIUS ANDREWS, a printer by trade, had homesteaded off South Bay by a creek later named Andrews Creek and filed a land claim on Sept 16, 1872. He and wife, Ada Cochell, had three children, all born in Grays Harbor. Their first child, Willis, arrived on October 1872. By 1880, the family had moved to San Francisco where his wife, Ada, a pianist, became influential in the development of the San Francisco Opera House. By 1900, Julius and Ada were divorced. Julius and sons relocated to Aberdeen. Mr. Andrews later became one of the first justices of peace and a highly-respected judge for his impartial decisions. He also built the Wishkah Mill in Aberdeen.[4]

Hoquiam's early school roster. Teachers:[5]

1873-74: Clara Nye
1874-75: Julia Andrew (Julius Andrews)

1875-77: Fannie Baldwin
1877-78: Mrs. M.B. Virgil
1878-79: Cornelia Newton
1879-80: Cornelia Newton
1880=81: Mrs. M.B. Virgil
1881-82: W.S. McCready

Hoquiam's school roster after the completion of Stevens School. Teachers:

1883-84: Ella Benjamin.
1884-85: Mary White
1885-86: A.W. Hutchins.
1886-87: Ada Sprague.
1887-88: Jessie Murch (resigned). Ola Gillespie.
1888-89: Teacher-principal: J.D. Dean
1889-90: J.D. Dean resigned as teacher. W.L. Adams appointed.

By 1890, Hoquiam was incorporated as a city and home to grocery stores, saloons, eateries, and hotels. With the attraction of immigrants to work in the mills and the woods, plus the speculation of the Northern Pacific Railroad extending its line, Hoquiam's population tripled from 400 to 1,500 as did the expansion of the city and property values.

In 1892, the three-story McKinley school was built and viewed as the architectural wonder of the growing town, but more than one teacher would be needed.

WHEN NETTIE CONNELL[1], twenty-four, arrived to Hoquiam in 1896, she had just completed a year of teaching at the rural school in Meacham, Oregon. She was also an 1894 graduate of the Weston Normal School in eastern Oregon.

NETTIE CONNELL
(Authors' collection)

---

[1] Nettie Connell, authors' great-grandmother.

NORMAL SCHOOLS SERVED as training schools for teachers and were already established in the East. With the influx of immigrants, the need for trained teachers was paramount and became a topic of discussion in Oregon by the mid 1870's. In other western states and territories too.

The courses of study, prepared by the president of each school and his board of trustees, followed the course of study of the first normal school in the United States at Lexington, Massachusetts, 1839. *These are the same courses Nettie completed during her three years at Weston.*

COURSE OF STUDY

- Orthography (*the conventional spelling system of a language*), reading, grammar, composition, rhetoric.
- Arithmetic (mental and written), algebra, geometry, bookkeeping, navigation, surveying.
- Writing, drawing.
- Geography with chronology, statistics and general history.
- Physiology
- Mental philosophy

<u>Hygiene</u>: Occasional short lectures on laws of health. Special attention to correct positions in sitting and standing.

<u>Drawing</u>: Daily drill in simple exerciser. (Hull's Exercises in the hands of the teacher.)

- Music.
- State constitution and history of the U.S.
- Astronomy.
- Natural history. The principles of piety and morality.
- The science and art of teaching with reference to all these subjects.
- In 1887, two years of Latin and one of Greek were offered.

By their senior year, normal-school students were teaching classes. At the Monmouth, Oregon school, each senior class member was required to teach twenty weeks, three hours per day. The Weston Normal School that Nettie attended more than likely followed a similar format.

NETTIE CONNELL ENROLLED at Weston, Oregon in 1891 at the age of nineteen. Shortly after her acceptance into the school, her parents sold their 160-acre farm in Albee, Oregon and purchased a 40-acre farm in Milton, ten miles from the school. Nettie, the eldest of thirteen children, eight still living, was the pride of the family and wherever she moved, they followed.

In 1896, before Nettie had gone to Hoquiam, the Connell family had sold the Milton farm and purchased the Starr Hotel in Sumpter, Oregon. A Sumpter newspaper describes the purchase and mentions that Nettie is teaching in Meacham but will be joining the family soon. It is believed that all, including Mastin Taylor who worked for the railroad in Meacham and was courting Nettie, thought she'd be teaching in Sumpter. Not only did her move to Hoquiam impact her family, but it contributed to the growth of Hoquiam's business community.

When Mastin Taylor arrived in 1898, he stepped into the role of a Hoquiam businessman, first managing Powell and Ross on Eighth Street, then opening his own store: The Economy Company (also called the Temple of Economy) and managing both. He also became a successful real estate investor and broker, a Hoquiam city councilman, and later opened the Taylor Produce Company on Levee Street.

(Authors' collection)

Nettie's sister, Agnes, came before the rest of the Connell clan, who had arrived in 1902. Agnes attended Hoquiam High School while Nettie was teaching. She worked in Mastin and Nettie's store and later married Harry Hubble, Hubble Tug Boats. Harry named one of his tugboats *"Agnes."* They had three boys: Harold, Hilland, and Howard.

Nettie's youngest brother, Ray, became a prominent businessman, owning the theaters: the Dream, the Arcade, and the Liberty, plus the Hotel New York, all in Hoquiam. The Weir and Connell Theaters were located in Aberdeen. One of his daughter's, Dorothye Logue (née Connell), became a Hoquiam school teacher at both Central and Lincoln Elementary Schools. After his passing in 1933, his second wife, Florence, also a teacher in Hoquiam, went back to teaching first grade at Central Elementary No. 2.

DURING THE END of Nettie's tenure at Meacham, she began sending letters to school districts, providing her credentials. When Hoquiam replied for her to come, it is unknown if it was for an interview or if she was hired unseen from her credentials, or once interviewed, hired on the spot. Nettie caught the steamship with direct passage to Hoquiam as she was also transporting her wardrobe trunk. It is known that after she arrived to Hoquiam she never returned to Oregon and moved into a Hoquiam boardinghouse. She immediately accepted a position to teach the seventh and eighth-grade classes at McKinley. The following year, Mastin Taylor and Agnes, Nettie's sister, arrived. Agnes moved into the boardinghouse with Nettie. Mastin moved into one several blocks away.

After the school term ended, Nettie and Mastin married on June 16, 1898. In some areas, women were not allowed to continue teaching after marriage, but in Nettie's case, they not only allowed it, but they promoted her to "Assistant Principal." Her duties expanded to not only teaching seventh and eighth grades, but ninth and tenth high-school courses too. She is pictured below with the 1898 graduating class.

1898 HOQUIAM HIGH SCHOOL GRADUATING CLASS
Back (LtoR):*Nettie Connell Taylor (Teacher/Asst Principal)*, Prof. Chamberlain (Superintendent) and Maude Richardson (Mrs. Winters) (Graduate)
Graduates seated (LtoR): Jessie Porter (Mrs. Stinchfield), Frankie Abbot or Albright (Mrs. Clark), Mary Richardson (Mrs. Crawford), and Edna Scott
(Courtesy of Larry R. Jones' collection)

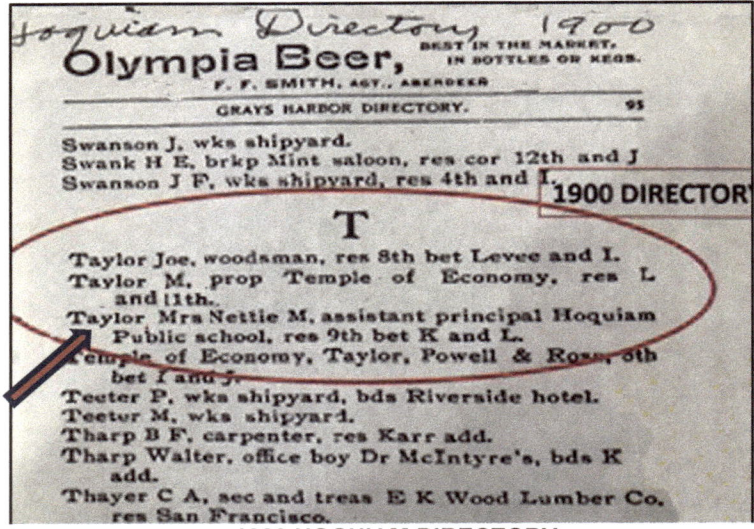

1900 HOQUIAM DIRECTORY
Mrs. Nettie Taylor listed as Assistant Principal Hoquiam Public Schools
(Courtesy of the Polson Museum)

NETTIE M. TAYLOR, ASSISTANT PRINCIPAL
P.A. Williams, Principal
(Authors' collection)

1899 REPORT CARD FILLED OUT AND SIGNED BY NETTIE
As Mrs. M. Taylor, teacher
(Courtesy of the Polson Museum, Hoquiam, Wash.
1995.010.0003-1 and -2)

Back of Card
Please inspect this report carefully, sign as indicated above and return promptly. We earnestly desire the cooperation of parents and guardians in our attempt to raise the standard of the school to the point where it shall be second to none of like grade.

Nettie continued with her teaching and principal roles through school term 1902. She worked for the Hoquiam school district for six years, but in 1902 was pregnant with her first child and forced to retire. They had three boys all with the middle name of Connell: Paul Connell Taylor, our grandfather (1902), Burton Connell Taylor (1904), and Homer Connell Taylor (1909). Young Paul started first grade at his mother's old school, McKinley, in 1909.

CHAPTER 3
OTHER SCHOOLS

COMMON SCHOOLS OUTSIDE OF the Hoquiam jurisdiction taught pupils common-school courses. If the student completed through the eighth grade after passing a final two-day exam, they would receive a Certificate of Graduation, which allowed the student to enter any high school without further examination. Such schools within the Hoquiam High School vicinity included Chenois Creek, also known as Fern Hill School.

CERTIFICATE OF GRADUATION—AGNES CLINE—MAY 28, 1919
Signed by: T.W. Bibb, County Superintendent
Ida Stilwell, Teacher
O.R. Burrows, Clerk of the Board of Directors
Josephine Preston, Superintendent Public Instruction
(Authors' collection)

Our grandmother, Agnes Taylor (née Cline), and her sisters, Viorene and Wilma, were raised along the Humptulips. To attend school, the sisters rowed a boat up Gillis Slough, then walked two miles on the railroad tracks. Before the building of Fern Hill School in 1912, a small cabin-like building on the west bank of Chenois Creek served as the school.

The Cline sisters were well versed on boats. Their father, Fred Cline, was a sea captain and a boat builder of seagoing steamboats as well as skiffs and rowboats. The girls learned to row by the age of five. Rowing to school, they would pick up other children along the way. Some of the Humptulips' families included: Bloom, Burrows, Chenois, Dunlap, Hunley, Merservey, Murphy, Nagel, Tanner, Whitcher, and Willis.

Agnes Cline, age 12, on Northern Pacific Railroad, the only road to Fern Hill School, 1915

**FERN HILL SCHOOL
(Chenois Creek)
1912-1923**
(Authors' collection)

The school attendance averaged between ten and twelve students, grades one through eight in one room with a potbellied stove. Water by pail with a dipper was filled each morning from the nearby creek, usually by the teacher or one of the older boys. There was an outhouse, but some of the boys used the woods instead.

The school put on several outdoor plays and the whole community showed up. In 1916, "Scrooge," with Clyde Chenois as the lead. During WWI, 1918, they performed a military drill to the music of "Under the Double Eagle," for the U.S. Army Spruce Camp at Grass Creek. (Pictured)

To receive a Certification of Graduation, eighth-grade students were required to take a two-day exam at Newton School, two miles from Fern Hill. Agnes Cline and Orin Burrows walked those two miles in the rain, then were peppered for two hours each day with questions, covering every subject. Agnes received her certificate on May 28, 1919.

Over the next four years she attended Hoquiam High School and rode the train to and from the Humptulips on Monday mornings and Friday afternoons, then rowed home. She stayed midweek with her grandmother, Lizzie Snyder, who lived in Hoquiam. She graduated from Hoquiam High School in 1923.

OTHER SCHOOLS

The Fern Hill school teachers were: Mrs. Holmes 1900-1912, Miss Mary Gleeson (McPhee) 1912-1914, Miss Verna Wheeler 1915-1917, Miss Pearl Pape 1918-1919, Miss Ida Stilwell 1919-1921. Miss Amada Jacobson (Kimball), 1922-1923, taught the last class at Fern Hill. The school was then abandoned. Wilma Cline was one of her pupils in that last class.

Agnes was interviewed by *Daily World* columnist Ade Fredericksen in 1990. Two articles later appeared in the newspaper: *Memories of Newton School* era and *Newton District had another school.*

**"UNDER THE DOUBLE EAGLE" MILITARY DRILL
US. ARMY SPRUCE CAMP, GRASS CREEK (During WWI 1918)**
Performed by "Fern Hill" School students.
Miss Pape's class (1918-1919)
**Several listed: VI (Viorene Cline), Agnes Cline, Clyde Chenois
Agnes Cline's handwriting at age 15, 1918**
(Authors' collection)

SPRUCE CAMP SOLDIERS
Davenport and Upton
**Hoquiam, Eighth and J Street,
Est. date 1918**
(Courtesy of the Polson Museum,
Hoquiam, Wash. 1984.038.0022)

MISS STILWELL (1919-1921)
(Authors' collection)

MISS AMANDA JACOBSON (1921-1923)
(Authors' collection)

Shortly after Miss Jacobson taught the last class at Fern Hill, the school was abandoned. She later married and by 1931 was teaching at the Newton School as Mrs. Kimball.

SEPTEMBER 1931, Gladys May lived at Chenois Creek and attended the Newton School for six weeks before returning to Emerson Grade School, Hoquiam. **Mrs. Amanda Kimball (née Jacobson)**, who once taught at Fern Hill School, was her teacher.

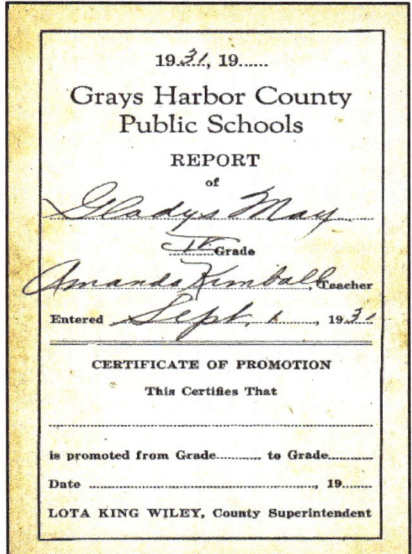

Grays Harbor County Public Schools (Rural) report card.
(Authors' collection)

NEWTON SCHOOL →

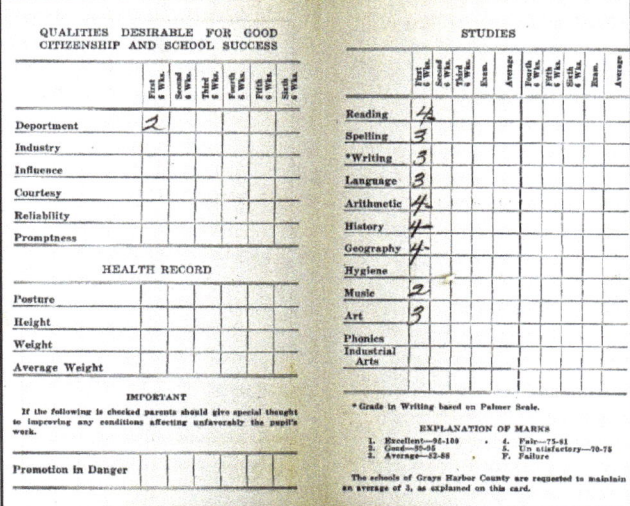

Any student who earned good grades got to bring in the fire wood and ring the school bell.

The Copalis Beach schoolhouse was built to this same floorplan.[1]

NEWTON SCHOOL
(Courtesy of Lee H. Thomasson's collection)

WITH RURAL SCHOOLS, like Fern Hill, children shared books. Many of the school books were furnished by the teacher during class and returned at the end of the session. Other times, the teacher would write lessons on the blackboard. The composition book was used by students to take notes as study guides.

AGNES CLINE'S 1916 (SIXTH GRADE) Composition Book
Fern Hill School,
Teacher: Miss Wheeler
(Authors' collection)

Agnes Cline's history notes:

Hamilton was born in the West Indies and was sent by friends to this country for an education. While a student at Columbia, Hamilton took part in the opposition to Great Britain. He joined the Army, was put on Washington's staff, and was in almost every battle.

BY 1919, AGNES was riding the rails between Hoquiam and Humptulips to attend Hoquiam High School as pictured (right).

THE BERNARD CREEK floating school house was placed by Asa and Mrs. Simpson by order from the Presbyterian trustees, 1890's. It served the NW Railroad camp, one mile west by trail in section 25. Later used by Bernard's

Camp and New London until a landed school was built just behind Valerio's Service Station. [m] Bernard and Chenois Creek schools were both in the Newton school district.

Agnes Taylor (née Cline) attended Bernard Creek for one week. Then later in 1915, she with her grandmother traveled there by steamboat for a spelling competition at the school. They walked ½ mile on the trail to reach it. Years later, Agnes showed her son, Paul, the location, between the railroad tracks and the bay.

In 2004, Agnes' son, Paul, was approached by homesteader Phillip Hunley who lived ¼ mile from Chenois Creek and whose family once attended Fern Hill School. "Do you know if a small grade school was there before Fern Hill School was built in 1912?" He asked. "Yes," Paul replied. "The float-house school was towed there by the Tug *Hunter* in the early 1900's. My mother, Agnes, at age six, attended it at Chenois Creek in the spring of 1909. There was no rain for March, April or May that year." [2]

It is assumed that the permanent Bernard Creek school that replaced the float-house school followed the same "Certificate of Graduation" process as Fern Hill, and that other rural schools like Newton and New London did too.

UPPER HUMPTULIPS AND NEW LONDON SCHOOL BUS (circa 1918)
(Courtesy of the Polson Museum, Hoquiam, Wash. 2007.003.0040)

Pictured are eighteen school children, one teacher, and school bus driver, Mr. Rosander.

---

[m] Bernard School. As told and documented by Paul B. Taylor from conversations with his mother, Agnes Cline Taylor (1903-1993), and his grandfather, Fred Cline (1874-1958). Paul B. Taylor, a historian and historical writer, was published in many magazines and local newspapers.

AS AN INFLUX OF immigrants arrived to the United States, public schools became the main institution teaching the immigrant children the English language and assimilating them into American culture and values. This created tradeoffs for the families, forcing them to surrender their heritage, language, and sometimes having to Americanize their names. [3]

With many nationalities working in the Grays Harbor mills and woods, schools specific to their heritage were erected by their community, such as the Finnish school pictured. Eventually, these children had to have integrated into Hoquiam's school system, but the process and time period is unknown.

FINNISH SCHOOL, 1905
(Courtesy of Polson Museum, Hoquiam, Wash, 2010.036.0246)

IN 1913, McKinley School was moved several feet to make room for the new Hoquiam High School. During this period, the McKinley school children were displaced. It is believed that this McKinley Annex was the temporary school location. [n]

MCKINLEY ANNEX SCHOOL, HOQUIAM (Circa: 1913)
Teachers: Miss Mathers, Miss Brown, and Miss Lenfesty
(Courtesy of Jones Photo Historical Collection L-00552_1)

---

[n] Based on 1950 census, Susan Lenfesty (AKA:Lenferty) taught mathematics. Susan, a 1904 HHS graduate, was one of the students who had signed the petition objecting the course-study change from physics to botany.

OTHER SCHOOLS

ST. MARY'S CATHOLIC SCHOOL (Hoquiam)
(Courtesy of the Polson Museum, Hoquiam, Wash., 1989.044.0016)

OUR LADY OF GOOD Help parish was established in Hoquiam in 1906 with a small church on Fourth Street. In 1907, the rectory was built, then a larger church in 1911. The parochial school (pictured) was constructed in 1920, followed by a convent in 1924. A parish hall and gymnasium were added in 1960. The school was closed in 1971 and later demolished.

IN THE MID 1950s, grades one through eight, were taught at the St. Mary's Catholic school by the nuns and the priest. Before enrolling, the students would attend kindergarten at one of Hoquiam's public elementary schools.

In addition to a religious education, the curriculum included science, mathematics, and language arts. The school also encouraged athletics. After the students completed eighth grade, they transferred into the ninth grade at Hoquiam Junior High. °

CATHOLIC EIGHTH-GRADE BASKETBALL TEAM (1965)
Eddie Logue, front row, second from left
(Courtesy of Eddie Logue collection)

° Eddie Logue, authors' cousin.

CHAPTER 4
RULES AND REGULATIONS

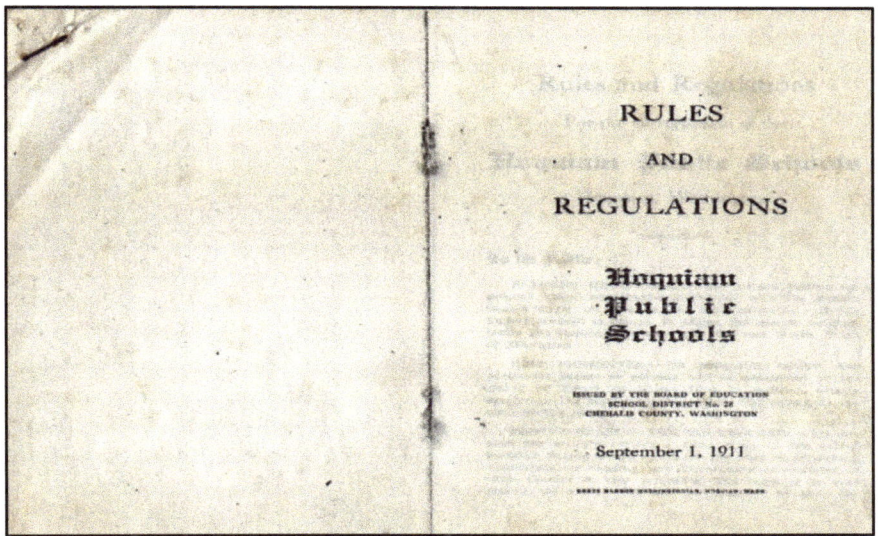

**RULES AND REGULATIONS
SEPTEMBER 1, 1911
HOQUIAM PUBLIC SCHOOLS**
(Courtesy of Larry R. Jones' collection)

WITH A NEW decade and a growing community, the Board of Education for School District No 28, Chehalis County, Washington, published a "Rules and Regulation" booklet for all teachers and administrators of the Hoquiam Public Schools, September 1, 1911.

Section 1: To the Public.

Processes for grievances:
- First contact the Superintendent. If not satisfied with the result, refer the case to the Board of Education.
- All complaints must be filed in writing, specifying the matter, and signed by the complaining party.
- All persons strictly forbidden to go to the school during school hours for the purpose of making a complaint or causing a disturbance.

Parents were invited to meet with the teachers to provide the best modes for discipline and instructions of their children. The booklet also stressed that the parents were to cooperate with the school authorities on the handling of such matters as: social amusement, business occupation, attendance, tardiness or absence by the student.

School Structure:
- Primary: first, second, third and fourth grades.
- Grammar: fifth, sixth, seventh and eighth grades.
- High school: ninth, tenth, eleventh, and twelfth grades.
- School started the first Monday in September and lasted thirty-eight weeks. It was divided into first and second semesters, each term nineteen weeks.
- Each semester was divided into three grading periods and the status of the student's progress was reported by the teacher to the superintendent and the pupil.

Telephone usage. Teachers nor pupils were to be called during school sessions, except for an urgent cause or sickness. Messages could be left. No pupil could use the telephone unless approved by the principal or teacher for urgent need.

Contagious diseases were a major concern. Smallpox, diphtheria, measles, and whooping cough, to name some. It was the duty of the teacher to make frequent inquiries in their classes whether there was sickness in the homes of their pupils and to report. Everyone associated: teacher, superintendent, janitor, pupil or family members were not allowed to attend school if they were living in homes where these diseases were prevalent. This included teachers who lived in boardinghouses. Readmittance to school required a certificate from a health officer or other registered physician.

TEACHERS

- Shall acquaint themselves with the rules and regulation of the schools, courses of study, and the plan adopted.

- Must be in their respective rooms at 8:30 a.m. and 12:45 p.m., and earlier if necessary.

- Expected to observe the light, ventilation, temperature, and cleanliness of their rooms and report any dereliction of duty of the janitor to the principal.

- Cannot dismiss pupils before the regular closing without the consent of the superintendent.

- Any teacher who is unavoidably absent must give immediate notice to the superintendent and to the principal.

- Must prepare themselves carefully, both as to matter and method, for conducting each school exercise in their respective departments.

- A daily exercise shall be prepared and followed, plus kept in a conspicuous place in the school room. A copy of the plan shall be sent to the superintendent within two weeks after the beginning of each term.

- During school hours, cannot send pupils on errands that do not pertain to school business.

- Shall maintain strict order and discipline in their rooms, in halls, on stairways, and on playgrounds. Any neglect in these matters, shall be considered good cause for dismissal.

- Excessive and unusual punishment shall not be inflicted. Corporal punishment shall not be administered except in the case of flagrant offense, when less severe modes fail to reform the pupil.

TEACHERS (continued)

- Shall require excuses from parents or guardians, either in person or by written note in all cases of absence, tardiness, or dismissal before the close of school. No excuse shall be deemed valid except that of sickness. Absences shall be placed in the hands of the attendance officer, who will investigate and enforce, if necessary, per school state laws.

- Must devote their energies to their school work and are not expected to assume, outside of school hours, social, business or household duties or responsibilities, which could impair their performance of school duties.

- Shall not detain pupils, as punishment, at the noon intermission, nor detain for more than thirty minutes after school, except by the permission of the principal.

- The superintendent shall evaluate the teacher's characteristics, relating to the lack of efficiency or effective teaching: insubordination or reluctant compliance, lack of sympathy or co-operation, absorption in social duties, frequent tardies and or rushing out of the building at the tap of the bell. Low ideal, antiquated methods, and lack of respect for the position and its pupils.

- Must keep a record of attendance, punctuality, deportment, and scholarship potential that is to be submitted to the principal on the first Monday following the close of a month.

- For the convenience of the superintendent, principal, substitute teachers, and visitors, must have a seating plan of the classroom and its occupants.

- Prior to receiving the last month's salary for the school year, the principal must receive all classroom keys from the teacher, plus completion of all required reports, and assurance that all desks and closets have been properly labeled.

RULES AND REGULATIONS

TEACHERS (continued)

- Teachers to be employed or re-elected for the next school year, must give the Secretary a written acceptance of the position within ten days after the receipt of notice. Failure to do so will be construed as declination.

- Any lady teacher who marries during the continuance of her contract must forfeit her position.

- Allowed ten days at half pay for sickness. If not at their classrooms at the specified time, shall suffer a deduction of one-fourth day's pay unless detained by sickness or urgent necessity. Teachers must report their own tardiness. If they are absent or tardy from meetings, they will suffer the same salary deductions, unless excused by the superintendent.

- Every teacher is empowered and enjoyed to command order on or about the school premises on the part of every pupil connected with the public schools.

PUPILS

- No pupil under six years of age shall be admitted to the public schools.

- Primary pupils entering school for the first time shall not be admitted after the second week of school. The Board could determine to admit the pupils during the first two weeks of the second semester.

- Pupils without promotion certificates from the Hoquiam public school, must report to the principal for classification.

- No pupil shall leave the school premises during school hours except by permission of the principal or the superintendent.

PUPILS (continued)

- Every pupil shall be punctual, regular in attendance, obedient to all rules and to the teachers, diligent, respectful, and kind and obliging to schoolmates.

- Willful disobedience, habitual truancy, vulgarity, or profanity, the use of tobacco, stealing, the carrying or using of dangerous playthings, and forging excuses, shall constitute good cause for suspension or expulsion from school.

- As soon as dismissed, pupils must leave the school premises and go directly home. Loitering on the way to or from school is forbidden.

- Must give attention to personal neatness and cleanliness. Any who habitually fails in this respect may be sent home to be prepared properly.

- Must pursue all branches to the grade or class they have been assigned, unless there are special reasons they are excused from the course by the superintendent upon recommendation of the teacher and principal.

- All pupils who fall behind in their class due to absence, irregular attendance, indolence, inattention or inability, shall be placed in the class below at the discretion of the principal, upon consultation with the superintendent.

- No teacher shall be allowed to excuse a pupil for absence or tardiness unless made by the proper parties, either in person or in writing. All excuses must state the reason.

- Pupils defacing or destroying property of school officials, shall make good for the damage.

- No pupil shall be allowed to retire from school during sessions, unless requested from proper parties in person or written request, unless an urgent matter arises.

THE ATTENDANCE OFFICER for the public schools exercised police powers in making arrests and in serving legal processes compliant with the new school code. They could enter stores, mills, shops or other places where children were employed to further their investigations for enforcement of the compulsory school law. They could take children between the ages of eight and fifteen, truant from school, into custody without warrant, taking them to their parents or directly to the school. (*Rules and Regulations, Hoquiam Public Schools, Sept 1, 1914. Duties of Attendance Officer, Pg 17-18; Section 11, 124, School laws, State of Washington.*)

TO PROTECT CHILD welfare, compulsory education laws were enacted in the United States around the turn of the nineteenth century. By 1918, every state had some form of compulsory attendances law on the books. Washington State's initial date was 1871.

JANITORS PLAYED AN important role in the schools. Most came from working-class backgrounds with little training of what it took to keep a school afloat. In addition to doing daily janitorial duties, such as: sweeping each room, hallways, stairways, restrooms, steps and closets, he had to keep the furnace running, and the building and windows pristine. Janitors worked unique schedules, usually alone from 3:30 p.m. to 8:30 a.m. on school days, Saturdays, and holidays, but were also on-call if a crisis arose.

Specific guidelines were enforced, such as abstaining from all liquors and tobacco while on the school premises and remaining out of the classroom thirty minutes after it was dismissed. They had to also take reasonable efforts to be agreeable to the teachers and the pupils. And always aware that any teacher had the authority to report on their work and demeanor.

The janitor fumigated all rooms and halls every three months, removed snow from steps and sidewalks, and kept the rooms at 70 degrees. He cleaned blackboards and erasers once a week, wound the clocks, kept the flag on display on all legal holidays and on school days, and rang the bell when the principal directed. For the janitor to clean a classroom, the teachers had to ensure that all papers were picked up off the floors, have the seats raised for sweeping, and when cleaning the boards, ensure that all crayons and erasers were removed. However, if these tasks were neglected, it more than likely would have been added to the janitor's list as he couldn't have left the classroom in an unfit order.

> WHENEVER THERE was an incident on the playground or in the classroom, the principal was summoned. During the early years, students would be whacked on the butt with a wooden paddle in front of the class. Later, the paddling occurred in the hallway outside of the classroom. Depending on the incident, the student might also be escorted to the principal's office for a lecture and/or a call to their parents. Through the years, the paddling device changed from a wooden paddle to a rubber sole of a tennis shoe.

Upcoming Chapters are by "Decades."

Decades—are periods of ten years, that begin with the Year "1" and end with the Year "0."

CHAPTER 5
A NEW DECADE
1911 THROUGH 1920

ON MAY 25, 1911, W.T. WALTON, the superintendent of the city schools, presided over the first meeting of the Hoquiam Alumni Association. The association's key purpose would be as an on-going ambassador for the school and the current graduating class. This would be achieved by boosting fundraising for scholarships, sponsoring events, and other necessary initiatives, plus acting as an advocacy group for important ballot issues concerning the school and the community. It was decided in this meeting that this organization would follow a formal alumni structure:

- Drafting a constitution
- Election of officers
- Set objectives
- Newsletters/Committees/Fundraising

During this first meeting, officers were elected, a constitution was drafted and adopted, and the first order of business was organizing a banquet in less than two weeks for the class of 1911. The banquet for the nine graduates was held in the dining room of the Hotel Grayport in Hoquiam. President E.A. Phibrick, Class 1894, of the association presided as toastmaster and master of ceremonies. The hotel was beautifully decorated and the graduates were pampered by members of the Junior class, acting as their servers. During dinner, the orchestra played and once eating stopped, the hall was cleared for dancing into variations of the waltz, which lasted well into the evening. (*The Hoquiam Alumnus* booklet, July 2, 1913, Pg 14, Authors' collection.)

Hotel Grayport

Leading Commercial and Tourist Hotel of Grays Harbor

First Class Cafe in Connection

Hours 7 a.m. to 1 a.m.

Special Sunday Table d'Hote Dinners

We solicit your patronage, and we make every effort to please you.

Class 1911: Caro Bruce, Geneva Foote, Gaynell Kellogg, Carrol Martin, Gladys Moan (née Smith), Faye Quaif, Hazel Renter, Minnie Stine, Ethel Bray (née Winkleman).

1911 WAS AN "ALL-GIRL" CLASS. The 1911 football team (below) were under classmates, who would be playing on the future teams of 1912 and 1913.

**1911 HOQUIAM FOOTBALL TEAM
SPORTING NEW SWEATERS**
(Courtesy of the Polson Museum, Hoquiam, Wash.
1977.067.0001)

The next year, 1912, thirteen students graduated from Central School. They were honored at two June events, both sponsored by the Hoquiam Alumni Association, with a committee chairman for each: Arthur Hunter, the ball and Lester Hanson, the banquet.

The second annual ball, held at the Electric Park, was also a fundraiser for future alumni initiatives, such as scholarships, and opened to all alumni of Hoquiam High School. The June 18th second annual banquet at the Hotel Grayport was strictly for the graduates and guest and stated to be as impressive as the one held for the class of 1911.

Class 1912: Ray Baker, Hazel Dawson, Harry Erickson, Freda Glover, Theresa Hegner, Morte Hunter, Ruth Karr, Kathryn McGlauflin, Mabel Smith, Sadie Sparling, Anna Stream, Ray Thurber, and Lois Williams.

BUT THE FOCUS ON EVERYONE'S MIND, was the prospect of a new high school. On November 23, 1912, a favorable election was held, securing $90,000 of bonds to build the new high school. The attorney-general's office, however, refused to approve, for the second time, the state's purchase of the bonds because of the small turnout of voters. Only 160 out of the 4,000 eligible had registered, and only sixty-three of those had voted, fifty-nine were for the bond and four against. Of the fifty-nine who had cast their affirmative vote, twenty-three of them were connected with the schools or were election officers.

The Hoquiam Alumnus publication, editorial column, featured all of these facts with this final statement:

> *The fault here lies with the people of Hoquiam, for to be sure, 59 citizens should not vote away $90,000 of public money for any purpose. But if another election were held, we believe that as a result of it, the attorney-general's office would hurry to approve these bonds, and that would put an end to the delay. Wherefore, in case another election is held, it should be the object of every alumnus of the high school to rise to the occasion with all possible aid, so that Hoquiam may have the advantages which the new high school offers.*[1]

The Alumni Association crusaded by word of mouth and door-to-door encouragement for all to register and vote! After another vote in late 1913, the new high school was a go.

THE CLASS OF 1913, with twenty-one members, was the largest in the school's history to graduate from Central School. They were touted as the brightest and best in all lines of school advancement.[2] Additional courses had been added that year: commercial and laboratory department, and the *Hesperian* staff had not only produced a superior book, but with good management, were able to pay off the old *Hesperian* debt and still sell the book at a lower price. Athletics and school spirit played a big part too. The freshman baseball team won the class championship and the junior class did the same in basketball. And to top it all off, the Hoquiam football team won the Southwest Washington football championship.

The third annual Alumni ball was held on June 26th at the Electric Pavilion in honor of the class of 1913. The large hall was decorated in the colors of the graduating class. Food and music were the best. Another banquet for the graduates was seven days later, July 2nd in the hall of the Hotel Grayport and followed a similar theme with decorations, a feast, and dancing to an orchestra.

Class 1913: Don Abel, Lena Abel, Grace Allman, Vincent Askey, Milton Baer, Orville Carpenter, Suzanna Cramer, Belle Cuthbertson, Elizabeth DeBush, Beatrice Fosdick, Erma Greosser, Ida Himes, Carolyn Hull, Marcus Jacobsen, Frank Martin, Wera Neick, Lora Powell, Marian Ross, Harold Rychard, Harry Shaneberger, Harold Stouffer.

OTHER EXCITING THINGS were happening in the community too. The Splash, advertised as Grays Harbor's annual Fourth of July celebration, July 3rd, 4th, and 5th, 1913, on the Hoquiam River, was to be the most successful exhibition ever held in the region. The program was to feature three events, the most amazing being the flights of Aviator Silas Christofferson, a daredevil who would be flying in one of his hydro-aero planes. Christofferson was to make five daily flights and a nightly exposition, dropping fireworks from his machine.

Included was the annual Splash with its aquatic attractions and contests, same as the year before (1912 pictured): log-rolling, swimming, canoe and boat races. "Skidroad, the Street of Many Attractions," was the third happening at this Splash event. (*The Hoquiam Alumnus*, July 2, 1913, Pg 4.)

THE SPLASH, FOURTH OF JULY HOQUIAM
Boat and Canoe races
(Authors' collection)

A NEW DECADE

THE NEW HIGH SCHOOL would be erected on Emerson Avenue and Garfield Street, but McKinley School had to be moved a short distance to make room.[3] Plans for the new high school had already been drawn up and approved. It would be as magnificent as McKinley had been viewed in its day.

Excerpts from *The Hoquiam Alumnus,* July 2, 1913, *The New High School, Pg 7,* (Authors' collection):

Hoquiam is to have a new high school which will not only benefit the school children but also add to the beauty of the city.

**HOQUIAM HIGH SCHOOL
1913-1914**
Building of the new school
(Courtesy of the Polson Museum)
(*Hoquiam High School 100 Years of Grizzly Pride!* Pg 7, booklet)

The dimensions over all are 173.6 by 109.6. The exterior will present an attractive appearance, the foundation of red brick, the main part of buff colored mottled brick, and the roof of slate. There will be chimneys, one at each end.

There will be two front entrances, one at the left and one at the right-hand side. Upon entering the right-hand side, there is a large locker running lengthwise of the building, cut off at each end by large corridors.

Upstairs, are two entrances to the large assembly room. This is 53.3 by 86.4. There will be a skylight all over the top of the assembly, which will extend to the top of the building. This room will seat about 300 pupils, this being about two and half times as many as the present assembly does. At the left-hand side of the assembly room there is to be a stage elevated about four feet, and measuring 26 by 13 ft.

The third floor is devoted entirely to the science department—chemistry, physical geography, botany, sewing and cookery.

53

The cookery and sewing laboratories were catered to teaching each girl all the necessities needed. They would also learn to wash and iron clothes.

BY JUNE, THE CLASS OF 1914 had graduated. It was the last class to graduate from the "Old Central" school. It is presumed that this class was honored by the Hoquiam Alumni Association as had been the tradition since they first organized in 1911. The 1914 class was also the first to publish a monthly *Hesperian*. This publication continued the next school year with the graduating class of 1915.

With the completion of the new high school, the Alumni Association stepped up with a dedication program. It is believed that this was one of their last actions as an organization. The committee included: President, Lester Hanson and members: Thayer Lamb, E.A. Philbrick, Ray Thurber, and Hubbard Tuttle.

HOQUIAM HIGH SCHOOL DEDICATION NOVEMBER 24, 1914
(Authors' Collection)

Note: Ray Thurber became a teacher and taught at Lincoln Elementary.[4]

In addition to the Board of Directors and faculty, the architects, builders, and superintendent of the construction were also honored. C. Howard French, the new principal replacing E.E. Davis, was also listed.

BOARD OF DIRECTORS

F. A. POWELL, President.
E. L. HURD, Vice-President.
SHERMAN HOOVER
D. M. OGDEN
K. C. BERG
HUBBARD TUTTLE, Secretary.

FACULTY

E. L. McDONNELL,	Superintendent
C. HOWARD FRENCH	Principal
BERTHA L. DAY	Music
RUTH M. WISE	History
CHARLOTTE HAASS	Languages
PERLE M. BATTLES	Botany
WILHELMINA HEIDEL	English
MARJORY MULLON	History
GEO. E. WILTSE	Commercial
F. E. SCHMIDTKE	Sciences
CORA SCHMALLE	Drawing
J. J. PENEPACKER	Arithmetic
HORTENSE EPPLEY	Domestic Science
A. J. BONHAM	Manual Training
JOHN E. EHRHART	Athletics

STEPHENS and STEPHENS	Architects
DITLEFSEN and GERRING	Builders
JOHN H. NEEF,	Supt. of Construction

**HOQUIAM HIGH SCHOOL DEDICATION
NOVEMBER 24, 1914 (Page 2)**
(Authors' collection)

SEPTEMBER 1914 WAS an exciting time at the start of the new school: modern desks, lockers, classrooms, all shiny and never used. The first graduating class of the new high school would be 1915, and the class of 1918 would be the first to go through all four years. Once again football led in school spirit. A full special edition of the monthly *Hesperian* highlighted the key players of the upcoming challenge between the Aberdeen and Hoquiam Thanksgiving game.

(L to R): top row: Bob Abel, Captain (Fullback), Dick Graham (Right Half), Allen Boyer (Left Half), bottom row: Dell McKinney (Quarter), Harold Narrance (Left End), Ronald Crawford (Left Tackle).

Other featured items were articles on the debate club with their two-year win as champions and the election of the Senior Class officers: Llewellyn Hartshorn, President, Allen Boyer, Vice-president, Lucile Blomquist, Secretary-treasurer, Robert Abel, Editor.

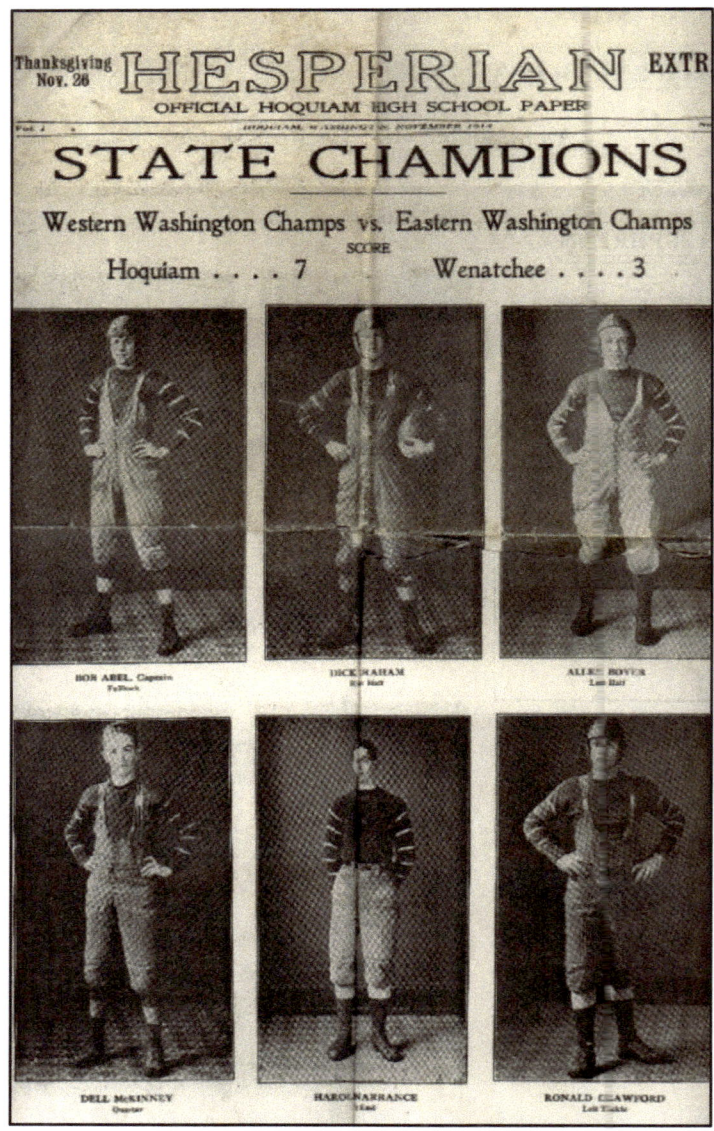

**HESPERIAN SPECIAL EDITION,
November 1914**
(Authors' collection)

With Europe at war in 1914, Lester plus other Harborites enlisted into the Navy Reserve. Some of their training was on ships in Grays Harbor. When the United States was pulled into WWI on April 6, 1917, many of these young men were shipped overseas, including Lester, who was stationed at the U.S. Naval Air Station, La Trinite, France through the end of 1918. **During the years 1917 through 1918, there was no football played at Hoquiam.**

**The Navy Unit above with Harborites
who enlisted into the Navy Reserve and were active in World War I.**
(Authors' collection, X Lester Hanson)
Note: Some of the young men were high-schoolers.

THE HOQUIAM ALUMNUS, July 2, 1913, Volume 1, Number 2, was the last published booklet of the 1911 Hoquiam Alumni Association. The biennial [p] booklet was twenty pages long at a cost of twenty-five cents a copy for pre-orders or fifty cents once published. Remittance was to be made to Lester Hanson.

The Directors of this 1913 publication were Ray Thurber, Class 1912 and Lester Hanson, Class 1909.

Officers: President: Thayer Lamb, Class 1892, Vice-Presidents: Mrs. Addie France, Class 1892 and Lester Hanson, Class 1909, Treasurer: A.G. Rockwell, Class of 1895, Secretary: Ray Thurber, Class 1912, Assistant-Secretary: Kathryn McGlauflin, Class 1912.

---

[p] Biennial occurs every two years or every other year.

The 1911 Hoquiam Alumni Association dissolved after the Hoquiam High School dedication in November 1914. It wasn't until fifty-six years later, 1970, that it reinstated as the Grizzly Alumni Association.

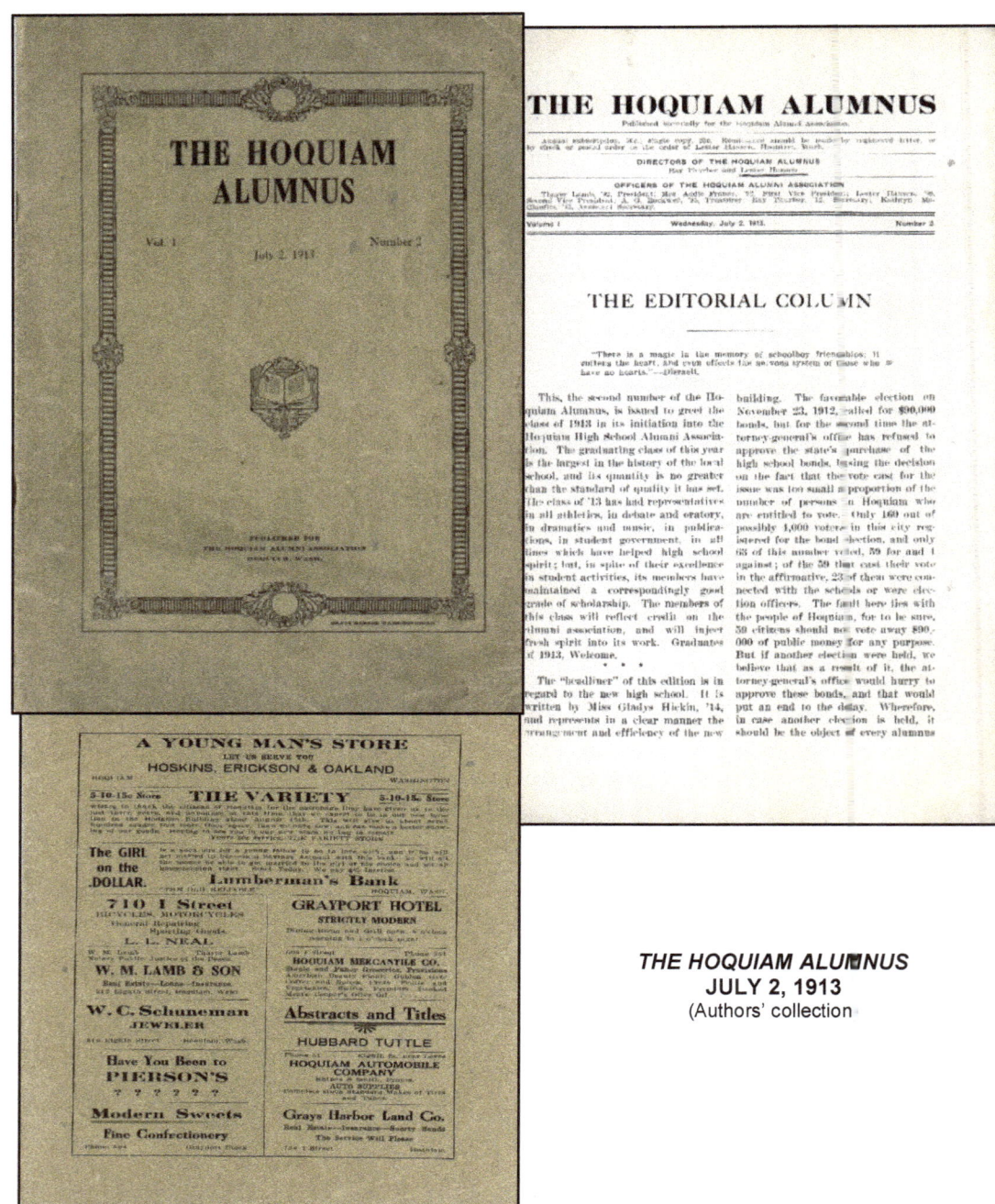

THE HOQUIAM ALUMNUS
JULY 2, 1913
(Authors' collection)

IN 1918, THIRTY-NINE had graduated, making this the largest in the history of Hoquiam schools. This was also the first class to complete all four years at the new high school and the first Hoquiam High School graduates to experience school life during a World War. Florence Snyder, half-sister to Lester Hanson, was one of those graduates.

Many of the high school girls belonged to the Patriotic League and Red Cross. To support their causes, they practiced Hooverization, which included monitoring their spending and limiting sweets.

Hoquiam students also purchased $12,000[q] of Thrift Stamps and War Savings Stamps. Their contributions were significant and could have been used to procure such items as: five hospital wards with twenty-five beds each or two machine guns or nine airplanes or nine motor trucks.[5]

War Savings Stamps were issued by the United States Treasury to help fund World War I. Unlike Liberty Bonds, largely purchased by financial institutions, the savings stamps were bought at the Post Office and promoted for the common man. They were interest-earning too.

To provide normalcy for the students, school traditions continued. With war looming, the Junior Class Prom, which was always organized by the Junior Class as a tribute to the outgoing seniors, was held.

The Junior Class
of the Hoquiam High School
requests your presence at their Prom
to be held at the Electric Park, Friday, February
the Sixteenth, Nineteen Hundred Seventeen
Dancing at nine o'clock
$1.00

(Authors' collection)

---

[q] $12,000 is about $213,000 in today's money (purchasing power).

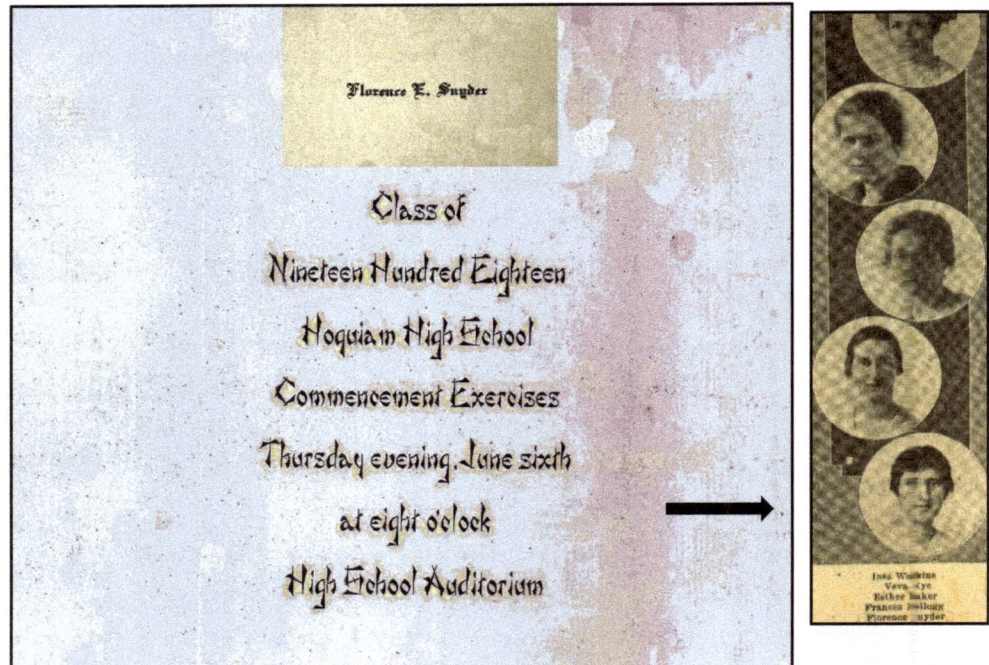

1918 GRADUATION ANNOUNCEMENT
Florence Snyder
(Authors' collection)

WHEN THE 1918 Spanish-flu Pandemic hit Washington State, Seattle was one of the first cities to implement restrictions: churches, businesses, and schools were halted and masks were mandated in all public operations. Once the virus reached Grays Harbor, Hoquiam followed a similar format, closing businesses and *all of the schools.* Local women were encouraged to enroll as nurses or as volunteers to help those with virus-stricken households.[6]

After graduation, Florence had enrolled in the U.S. Student Nurse Reserve program, which required a Certificate of High School Study signed by Principal Bonham and certified by the Council of National Defense. She plus other graduates volunteered at the local Red Cross. With a second uptick of cases erupting in early December 1918, the Red Cross opened an emergency hospital in the Eagles Hall on Seventh and J Streets.

The schools reopened in 1919. The graduating class had grown smaller, only thirty-six. Many of the boys had enlisted in 1917.

---

[r] Florence Snyder, authors' great-aunt.

After a two-year hiatus, Hoquiam sports was reinstated. Boys and girls were now being encouraged to sign up for their elective teams: basketball and football, to name a few favorites. In November, the Hoquiam and Aberdeen Thanksgiving Day game was resumed, but due to Hoquiam's two years of inactivity, they suffered a large defeat of thirty-three to six.

That same winter, students, who lived up the east fork of the Hoquiam River, were having difficulties getting to school on time. To remedy the problem, the school district purchased an additional boat. [7]

The class of 1920 formed committees for a special school event, not only to keep school spirit high, but to make money for the publication of the *Hesperian*. The event name chosen: "Hokum Hikus Sirkus," was advertised on posters drawn by talented classmate Otto Eklund and plastered all around town with the help of Roberta Smith.

"Hokum Hikus Sirkus," held for two nights on March 5th and 6th, 1920, featured two fortune telling booths: "Mutt and Jeff" and "The Passing Show." Both shows were put on by the junior class. The sophomores hosted an ostrich farm, and the freshmen class peddled large quantities of ice cream. Home Economics sold lemonade, candy, and tarts.

The main show was Mr. Narrance and Mr. Johnson, two famous boxers, giving an exhibition on skates. Three hundred people attended the carnival. Six-hundred dollars was earned, five hundred of it was given to the *Hesperian*.

**1920 *HESPERIAN*
Hokum Hikus Sirkus**

CHAPTER 6
THE 1920s
(1921-1930)

THE 1920s BECAME an exciting decade. Hairdos and fashions were changing as were the attitudes of careers for young women. Hoquiam High School's Commerce Department stepped up to the challenge. Hoquiam was the only school in the county providing advanced work in typewriting and shorthand.[1]

The fourth semester of the two-year shorthand course had been turned into an office-practice class, teaching the adding machine and stenciling, plus other office related tasks. Some of the girls worked at the front desk in the office, checking excuses and attendance and taking long distance telephone calls.

By 1928, the typewriting department had thirty-two machines that were in constant use during class and after school too. This same year, Hoquiam was represented at the Centralia Southwestern Typewriting contest, the state contest in Seattle, and at the Grays Harbor County contest in Montesano. Dorothy McCulloch won the county contest, earning a prize of two five-dollar gold coins.

HOQUIAM HIGH SCHOOL TYPEWRITING CLASS (Above) and OFFICE PRACTICE CLASS ➡ 1921 *Hesperian*

Other Commerce Department courses included bookkeeping and mechanical drawing. Across the street at Central No. 1, students were perfecting their penmanship.

HOQUIAM JUNIOR HIGH SCHOOL PENMANSHIP CLASS
(Central No. 1—grades seventh and eighth)
1921 *Hesperian*

HOQUIAM HIGH SCHOOL MECHANICAL DRAWING CLASS
1921 *Hesperian*

EMERSON GRADE SCHOOL 1922.

Emerson Grade School, named after George H. Emerson, was built in 1922 for the children who lived on the west end of town. It is located on the cross streets of Emerson Avenue and Adams and is the last of the early Hoquiam schools on its original site.

EMERSON GRADE SCHOOL 1922
(Courtesy of the Polson Museum archives)

IN THE MID-1920s, school traditions continued, such as the carnival "Hokum Hikus Sirkus," which was renamed "Hokum Silly Sirkus." Hoquiam High School had procured a moving-picture machine and began showing movies, and the annual "Bean Feed" was still being held.

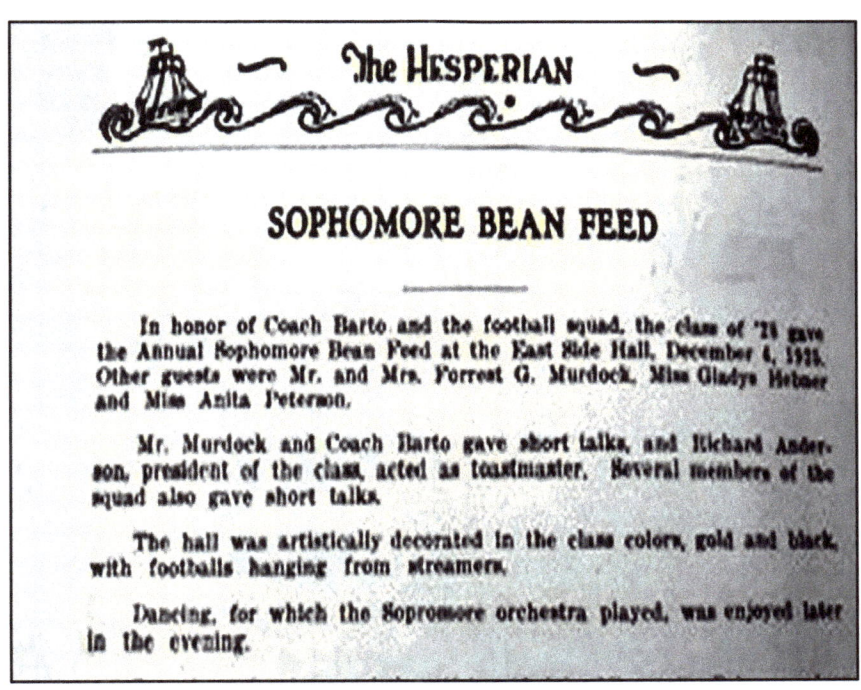

DECEMBER 4, 1925 BEAN FEED

THE BEAN FEED was first started in 1907 by the Sophomore maidens wanting to honor the boys in their class. They prepared a special feast with a main course of beans followed by bean pickles (pickled green beans, perhaps) and candy beans, a jelly-bean type confection, for dessert. Later, the boys were obliged to bow to a loaf of bread, which got passed down the next year to the Class of 1908. It is unknown how many times this loaf resurfaced.

The Bean Feed was later revamped. It was still sponsored by the Sophomores, but now included the entire class, both boys and girls. Their mission was to prepare a dinner of beans for an organization or team whom they deemed deserved this honor. Sometimes the senior graduating class received the bean-feed honor as reflected in the 1913 picture. The feed was always held at a hall or hotel and decorated in the class colors of the Sophomore Class.

THE ANNUAL BEAN Feed of 1921 was held on November 25 at the New York Hotel. The banquet room was decorated in the 1922 Sophomore class colors of purple and white. The honorees were the football lettermen. Howard Philbrick was the toastmaster. Following the dinner, the party moved to the American Legion Hall for the Bean-Feed Dance.

HOQUIAM HIGH SENIORS (Central No. 1)
1913 BEAN FEED RECIPIENTS
(Courtesy of the Polson Museum, Hoquiam, Wash. 2016.060.0046)

The Bean Feeds continued throughout the 1920s. The one sponsored by the 1928 Sophomore class was held on December 4, 1925 at the East Side Hall to honor Coach Barto and the football squad. The hall was garnished in the 1928 Sophomore Class colors of gold and black with footballs hanging from the streamers. Music for the dancing was played by the Sophomore orchestra.

PICTURED ON THE steps of the old McKinley school is the 1925 Hi-Y club. Later that same year, McKinley was razed to make room for the construction of the new Hoquiam Junior High.

**1925 HOQUIAM HIGH SCHOOL
"HI-Y CLUB"**
Forming a "Y" on the McKinley Steps
1925 *Hesperian*

THE HI-Y CLUB boys were chosen each year from the Junior and Senior Class for creating, maintaining, and extending, throughout school, high standards of Christian living.

They sponsored assemblies for the student body, the bonfire and rally before the annual Thanksgiving football game. They also entertained during basketball half-times and organized informal and formal dinners.

WITH THE CONSTRUCTION of the new Junior High building (1925-1926), Hoquiam realigned its middle-school grade levels, which now encompassed seventh, eighth, and ninth grades. Prior to this, ninth grade was the first entry into high school.

**HOQUIAM JUNIOR HIGH SCHOOL, 1926
On the old McKinley School site**
(Courtesy of the Polson Museum,
Hoquiam, Wash.2011.023.0004)

Junior High Control Board
Richard Hopkins, Louise Knoell, Robert
Matheson, Maxine Morrow
and Junior Dean (two unidentified)
1927 Hesperian

In the fall of 1926, the future class of 1930 entered the new Junior High as freshmen.[2] Some of the seventh and eighth grade classes, maybe all, remained at Central No. 1 across the street. This new building also housed the Superintendent and the Junior High School principal as well as administrative staff. The Superintendent occupied the arched half-window office at the front.

Excerpts (1927 *Hesperian*):

Our new building (Junior High School) was completed in time for the opening of school in the fall (September 1926) and school days recommenced with a bang.

The new Junior High auditorium was christened by the first senior-high debate and has since rung with the victories of the junior-high team.

68

In basketball, we were very successful, winning every league game and bringing home the pennant. The classes of '30, '31, and '32 have every reason to be proud of their 1927 basketball team.

JUNIOR HIGH BASKETBALL

During this period, Central No. 2, next door, was in its final phase of completion. Central No. 2 replaced McKinley as the elementary school for grades one through six, for those living within the central perimeter of town. Kindergarten was later added in the early 1940s, making it one of the first public-school kindergartens in Hoquiam.

CENTRAL No. 2, 1926
(Courtesy of the Polson Museum,
Hoquiam, Wash.2013.046.0040)

IN 1928, THE "GRIZZLY" was chosen as the high school mascot. Prior to this, the Hoquiam team was called the "Crimson and Gray."

THE GRIZZLIES 1928 →

THE GRIZZLIES
On the muddy Emerson Field

1929 CLASS POEM

We are leaving our old Hoquiam high school
And going forth to join in the stride.
We will work in the highest places,
And will look for the best in life.

Some will go to lands far distant,
And with strangers make their home.
Others on a world of water,
All their lives, chance to roam.

But whatever may be our destiny.
When we think of our high school days,
We'll remember every classmate,
With our hearts full of honor and praise.

It was only four short years ago,
We gathered at our meeting,
To choose our colors and motto
"Be square" was our high school greeting.

Let's keep this motto in our hearts,
All through our work and play.
Isn't that what we chose it for?
To be kept in practice every day?

Underclassmen since we are leaving,
Some advice we give to you:
Use our motto in your school work,
It will help to pull you through.

When our way is burdened with care,
And our life seems full of tears,
We'll look back with fond recollection
On our happy high school years.

Dorothye Rae Connell

Dorothye Connell—"Dot" is keen as feature editor of the High Life. She is always vivacious and sparkling with snappy greetings for everyone.

---

s Dorothye Rae Logue (née Connell) taught school in Hoquiam for over twenty-five years at both Central and Lincoln. Dorothye Logue, authors' cousin.

1930 GRADUATING CLASS would be the last of the roaring-twenties decade, and sadly, the first to experience the largest financial crisis of the twentieth century. October 29, 1929, Black Tuesday, hit the stock market and plummeted the nation into a deep depression, which lasted through the next decade.

CHAPTER 7
THE DEPRESSION YEARS
(1931-1940)

THE GREAT DEPRESSION, as it was termed, brought new pressures to the schools. School supplies were monitored, textbooks preserved, and teachers' salaries frozen. Many of the students' families were facing financial peril. The lumber industry was in a downward spiral which rippled throughout Grays Harbor County.

It is unknown when kindergarten first filtered down to Hoquiam, but it was during these Depression years that kindergarten was being held in private homes with a class size of ten or so. Kindergarten wasn't a new teaching practice, in fact, it dated back to Friedrich Froebel who established the first kindergarten in Blankenburg, Germany in 1837.

Froebel described children as plants and teachers as gardeners. Kinder in German meant child and garten meant garden. In his school, he emphasized play, starting with simple activities, then progressing to more complex games. He spent ten years perfecting his concept and created what he referred to as gifts, such as educational toys, songs, and finger plays. Kindergarten arrived to the United States in 1848. Elizabeth Peabody opened the first English speaking kindergarten in Boston, Massachusetts in 1860. In 1873, the expansion of kindergarten began with Peabody corresponding with William T. Harris, Superintendent of the St Louis public schools. By the 1900s, kindergartens were viewed as a community center for the neighborhood. [1]

By 1914, every major city in the United States had established at least one public kindergarten. The Seattle Emerson Elementary, founded in 1909, was the first public kindergarten in Seattle.

THE OBJECTIVE FOR the Hoquiam kindergartens in the early 1930s was for the children to interact and to adjust to being away from home. No academics were taught. Instead, the children sang, drew and colored, played games, and listened to stories read by the teacher. Weather permitting, they also had playtime outside, plus birthday parties and a Christmas program.[2] These classes provided a happy distraction for the children and an income for families who hosted them, but were only available to those whose families could afford to pay. By the mid-1930s a more structured kindergarten, accommodating twenty-five or so students, was held in the basement of the Christian Science Church on L Street in Hoquiam. It is unknown if this was also a private fee-based class or specific to the children whose family followed the Christian Science religion. It was taught by Mrs. Krekow, who went on to be one of Hoquiam's public-school kindergarten teachers for years to come.[3]

SUPERINTENDENT CRUMPACKER kept the Hoquiam School District afloat by putting all of Hoquiam's public schools on a cash basis. As a result of his efforts, the high school doubled its athletic and educational facilities. Modifications were made to events and publications. For one, the annual Bean Feed was replaced with a Sophomore Dance. The *Hesperian* cut corners too, such as the example of the 1936 yearbook with the comb binding.

In 1932, the *Hesperian* was in jeopardy of not being published. The Hoquiam businessmen, merchants, and school classmates pulled together to make it happen.

The school newspaper minimized its publication to a few pages and adopted the name "Squirrel Bait." It was later renamed "Hi-News" in 1936.

ON DECEMBER 19, 1933, THE *Washingtonian* reported: "A terrific storm Sunday morning, coupled with badly swollen rivers and high tides, brought the highest waters in Grays Harbor's history."

Civil work crews, financed by the federal government, were cutting additional outlets to offset incoming tides. Ninety-mile gale winds had ripped tin roofing from roofs and live wires caused

HOQUIAM 1933 FLOOD
(Courtesy of Polson Museum
Hoquiam, Wash., 2021.023.0760)

havoc to workers. People were being rescued by boats. Superintendent Crumpacker reported water in the Hoquiam High School basement and closed all of Hoquiam's public schools. [4]

TO KEEP SPIRT high during the Depression, various high-school clubs were formed: an archery club, the pep club, and a broadcasting club, plus others.

For the broadcasting team to earn points, reporters had to submit five stories each month. A typist typed at least ten pages and announcers had to broadcast for twenty minutes.

The Marksmen Club, organized by Mr. Chapple, required its members to construct their own bows. Native yew wood for the bows was procured from local forest near the small beach communities of Aloha and Carlisle.

An archery range was erected in the high school gymnasium and open for practice every Monday, Wednesday, and Thursday evenings. Doris Henderson kept records of all of the practice shots.

THE MARKSMEN CLUB
(Archery)

THE YELL KING, who usually wore white, became a staple at all of Hoquiam's high school events. Accompanied by two male assistants, the yell king was always the main focus leading the cheers, cartwheels, and other acrobatic stunts. The Yell King was also one of the student body officers and a member of the Board of Control. He, however, appointed his

1931 HOQUIAM YELL KING HERB GRANT
With assistants Bob Beaudoin and Paul Fredrickson

own yell assistants. The 1931 Yell King, Herb Grant, was also a football player, so had a double duty to perform that year. He had always been famous for his life and energy throughout his four years of high school. With the assistance of Bob Beaudoin and Paul Fredrickson, Grant was able to accomplish this task.[5]

In addition to entertaining at the games, assemblies, and rallies, a "yelling," competition occurred between the Aberdeen and Hoquiam students at the annual Thanksgiving game. As a result, the two schools agreed to award a trophy to the school whose students cheered the loudest at three consecutive Thanksgiving games. Hoquiam won two years in a row.

At the deciding third year of 1936, cheering and stomping pulsated through the stands, until suddenly, without warning, the Aberdeen grandstand collapsed beneath their feet! It is unknown if anyone was hurt, but can be assumed that the contest never resumed.[6]

Song queens later joined the ranks of the cheering team. They were voted in by the school board and student body.

Initially song queens lead the schools in songs, while the yell king and assistants performed acrobatics and influenced the cheers.

HOQUIAM SONG QUEENS WITH YELL KING ➔

IT WAS DURING the 1930 Depression that the Hoquiam High School band was formed. Prior to that, Hoquiam only had an orchestra and choir. The band boosted school spirit for both the students and the community with patriotic and energetic tunes, plus marched at games and in local parades.

IN 1933, THE *USS CONSTITUTION*, also known as *Old Iron Sides* stopped at Grays Harbor on her three-year, 90-port tour. The Hoquiam High School Band attended the ceremony and played a patriotic tune.

During the ship's restoration, Hoquiam's elementary children had collected money and mailed their funds to Boston. This may have spearheaded Grays Harbor to be chosen as one of her stopping ports.

> **Excerpt from the NEA-Boston Bureau newspaper, 1930 (See References at the back for the full article):**
> Pennies contributed by school children in **Hoquiam** and other American communities made possible the reconditioning of the historic frigate, pictured here as it was set afloat at the Charleston, Mass. Navy yard after being under construction for three years.

The ship was launched in 1797 from Boston, and was and still is, the world's oldest commissioned naval warship. Her name was chosen by President George Washington. She earned her nickname, *Old Iron Sides,* during the 1812 battle with the British warship, *HMS Guerriere.*

HOQUIAM HIGH SCHOOL BAND
On the deck of "*OLD IRONSIDES*"
(Courtesy of the Polson Museum, Hoquiam, Wash.
2006.012.0003)

IN 1936, HOQUIAM'S championship band won highest honors at the Southwest Music Festival and was invited to march in the Portland Rose Festival parade.

**HOQUIAM HIGH SCHOOL
MARCHING BAND
April 1936, Dedication of the Eighth Street Bridge
Reopening**
(Courtesy of the Polson Museum, Hoquiam, Wash.
2001.042.0009)

1936 *Hesperian* write up:

TO THE BAND must go the honor of being just about the most popular organization, and at the same time, the hardest working group in school.

The **bandmen** accompanied the football squad to all their games, played at all home basketball games, and created pep in student-body programs.

As a civic organization, the group has become very popular They presented concerts at the Hoquiam and Aberdeen Elk's club, played at the Hoquiam Merchant's Exposition, and participated in many school activities.

To climax a successful year the band under the direction of E. Ronald Rice, won the highest honors at the Southwest Washington music meet staged at Vancouver.

A public concert was given by the band in May and seemed to be much appreciated. Many invitations to play have been received, but bandmen look forward with greater eagerness to participation at the Portland Rose Festival to be held sometime in June.

On April 26-27, 1940, twelve-hundred musicians attended the Southwest Washington music meet at Hoquiam High.

**1939-1940 HOQUIAM HIGH SCHOOL
MARCHING BAND**
(Courtesy of the Polson Museum, Hoquiam, Wash.
2006.036.0002)

MISS BLACK founded the Hoquiam Pep Club in 1934. Their purpose was to arouse interest in school activities. On game day and for rallies, the Pepsters sported their crimson sweaters inscribed with a large "H".

HOQUIAM PEP CLUB (1934)

Excerpt from the *Hesperian*:

AS ITS NAME implies, the Pepster Club has only one purpose—that is to create that certain something called "pep."

On that day when even the most placid club member becomes slightly pugilistic, or in other words on Thanksgiving Day, the Pepsters made their debut. Aside from marching between halves of the grid-contest, the girls thought of the original idea of selling miniature footballs with crimson and gray ribbons attached. No doubt these Pepsters wore their rabbit foots as well, for the outcome was 13-0 in our favor.

THE 1936 *HESPERIAN* was dedicated to Superintendent Crumpacker. In addition to keeping the school district solvent through the Depression, he had saved sufficient funds to add a new gym and an entire new wing of classrooms.

NEW BUILDING ADDED, 1936
Behind high school
(Courtesy of the Polson Museum, Hoquiam, Wash., 2007.011.0007)

PRESIDENT FRANKLIN D. ROOSEVELT on his 1937 Olympic Peninsula tour.

PRESIDENT ROOSEVELT'S MOTORCADE, 1937
Passing Hoquiam High School
(Courtesy of the Polson Museum, Hoquiam, Wash., 2007.011.0008)

Florence Connell

FLORENCE CONNELL[†] TAUGHT first grade at Central Elementary No. 2 for school term 1933-1937. Her son, Ray, was in her 1937 first-grade class. This was Ray's first year of school, there was no kindergarten at Central No. 2 at that time. His recollection of President Roosevelt's visit:

> "My mother taught first grade at Central Elementary. Her first-floor classroom was to the right of the front door with the series of windows facing the street. The building next door, which sat between the high school and Central, housed the Superintendent's office. It had an arched half-window toward the top and the office was painted, I believe, a greenish hue.
>
> When President Roosevelt came through Hoquiam on his Olympic Peninsula tour, all the children were given tiny flags. As we stood on the curb watching his motorcade pass, we waved our miniature flags back and forth." (K. Taylor interview with Cousin, Ray Connell 1/22/24.)

[†] Florence Connell, authors' great-aunt by marriage.

THE DEPRESSION YEARS

THE YEAR 1939 PROVED a fruitful one for Hoquiam High School sports. Boxing had been introduced the prior year and became a major interest to many boys wanting to learn under the fine coaching of A.E. Bargewell.

Coach Elmer Huhta, a 1924 Hoquiam graduate, was one of the first local coaches to win three championships in a row. In 1931, he became the new head football coach. The next year, 1932, he took the Grizzlies to a Southwest title with a tie for state champs. In 1933 the team was undefeated. From 1934 through 1936, the Grizzlies went on to win their three consecutive state championship crowns. In 1939, he took the reins of the basketball team and led them to their first of two state championship titles.

Excerpts from a 1965 news article:

For eleven rollicking years, Southwest Washington and much of the state danced to Elmer's tune...

Fifteen years have gone by since the Grizzlies last nailed a football or basketball pennant only.[7]"

HOQUIAM 1939 BASKETBALL STATE CHAMPIONS
Elmer Huhta (Coach), Second from Right, head turned.
(Courtesy of the Polson Museum, Hoquiam, Wash. 1980.061.0002)

HOQUIAM HIGH SCHOOL BATON TEAM
(Hesperian)

BY THE LATE 1930s, baton twirling had taken hold for young girls. Hoquiam High School had formed a baton team to entertain at half time and parades. Pictured, is the baton team in formation with the head majorettes as leads.

CHAPTER 8
WORLD WAR II YEARS AND AFTER
(1941-1950)

BY 1940, World War II had broken out across Europe after Nazi Germany invaded Poland in late 1939. Germany, Italy, and Japan had signed a joint military and economic agreement. Germany then invaded its European neighbors: Belgium, the Netherlands, France, Denmark, Norway, Luxembourg, Romania, and began continual bombing of Great Britain.

Americans didn't want another war, so the United States shifted to a "nonbelligerency" with a lend-lease act, which allowed material aid to the allies in exchange for 99-year leases on property for foreign military bases. This kept the United States out of the conflict until December 7, 1941, then everything changed:

– December 7th, the Japanese attacked Pearl Harbor.
– December 11th, Germany and Italy declared war on the United States.
– Shortly after, the United States declared war on them.
– **January 1942, the first American troops arrived in Great Britain.**

IN 1942, THE GIRLS' LEAGUE conference at Battle Ground could not be attended because of the tire shortage. Due to gas rationing, out of town trips, like music meets, were cancelled. Instead, the Hoquiam High School choir, under director Mr. Salyer, performed at various local events: the Elks, the Eastern Star and Saron Lutheran Church, and the Christmas assembly, plus four concerts, an Army Relief show at the Seventh Street Theater, and an Easter Sunrise service. The choir lost count on the number of performances that "The Ballad for Americans," an American Patriotic Cantata,[u] was performed.

---

[u] Cantata, medium-length narrative piece of music.

BEFORE COACH HUHTA enlisted into the Air Force in 1942, he led the basketball team to their second state championship title. After the war, he returned to Hoquiam to teach school.

1942 BASKETBALL STATE CHAMPIONS
(Courtesy of the Polson Museum, Hoquiam, Wash. 1980.061.0007)

ON DECEMBER 22, 1942, Congress passed an amendment to the U.S. Flag code to remove the flag salute, instead, the right hand would now remain over the heart. All schools immediately followed the mandate, starting with the grade schools whose students quoted the *Pledge of Allegiance* every morning.

Previously while reciting the pledge, the hand was placed over the heart. When the word, *flag*, was reached, the right arm was then extended straight toward the flag until the pledge was finished. It parallelled the Nazi salute.

The pledge and salute were created in 1892 off of a campaign by *Youth Companion* magazine to have the American flag placed in every classroom. The magazine owner, Daniel Ford, tasked his staff writer, Francis J. Bellamy, to come up with a mantra to encourage patriotism, which resulted in the pledge. It was determined that a gesture was needed, thus the salute.

This change caused confusion for many, especially for the elementary schoolchildren, who had been executing this salute every morning. [1]

DURING THE WAR, the high school sponsored noontime movies, dances, and the University of Washington forum speakers. Book drives and War Stamp sales were launched as well as the Victory Corps.

The Victory Corps provided military training to male and female high-school students. Their objectives were to train the youth for war service after they left school, and while in school, to engage their active participation in their community's war efforts. Their training focused on both physical conditioning as well as specific academics needed for the selected armed service branches the student wished to pursue, such as science and mathematics.

Same as what had happened twenty-four years prior during WWI, the country was asked to buy War Stamps to help pay for the war. Once a book was filled, which cost $18.75, it could be traded for a War Bond that would be worth $25.00 in ten years. Rationing was also started. Sugar came first, followed by gasoline and shoes. Over the next few months, more ration books were issued. Each member of the household would receive two books. [2]

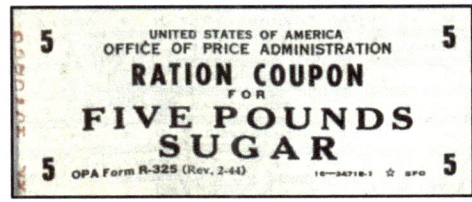

(Authors' collection)

ONCE THE WAR was declared, all men received a draft status. Eligible men were immediately drafted. Fathers were exempt.[3] A number of Hoquiam High School boys were inducted into the armed forces, leaving few to participate in high-school sports.

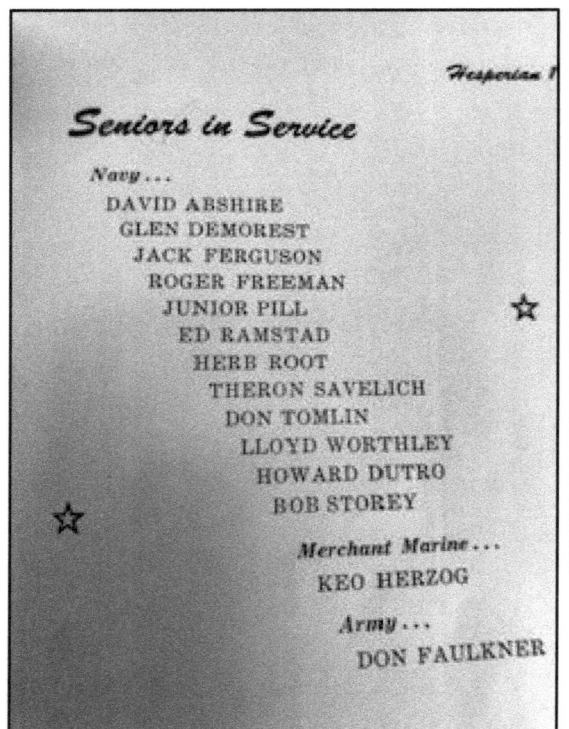
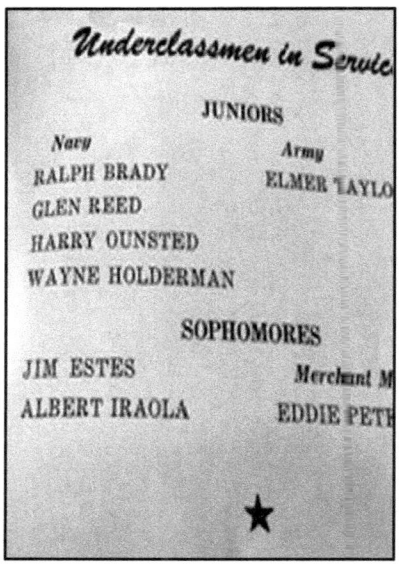

1943 HESPERIAN

By 1943, the band had lost seven members to the armed services. The concerts were held on school nights instead of Sunday afternoons because of fuel rationing. The first concert was held in February and well received with almost full-seating capacity. In a contest between the brass and woodwind section for ticket selling, the woodwinds won and were fed a dinner in the school cafeteria.

DEDICATION FROM THE CLASS of 1943 to the under classmates of Hoquiam High: We, the class of 1943, bequeath to you, graduation ceremonies undimmed by war clouds—a class day with no vacant chairs—a senior picnic unhampered by worries of tire rationing—and a commencement when hopes of graduating members have every chance of being realized in a democratic world.

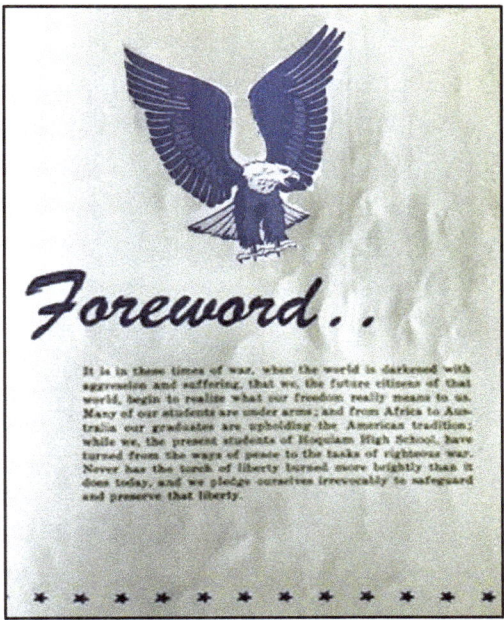

IT IS IN THESE TIMES OF WAR, when the world is darkened with aggression and suffering, that we, the future citizens of that world, begin to realize what our freedom really means to us. Many of our students are under arms, and from Africa to Australia our graduates are upholding American tradition; while we, the present students of HOQUIAM HIGH SCHOOL, have turned from the ways of peace to the tasks of righteous war. Never has the torch of liberty burned more brightly than it does today and we pledge ourselves irrevocably to safeguard and preserve that liberty.

1943 *HESPERIAN*

IN THE BEGINNING of the war, blackouts became a regular occurrence. People hung blankets or cardboard over their windows. Some even painted their windows black. Later, Selden Furniture and Carpet Company started producing and selling blackout blinds.

Prior to the 1941 Pearl Harbor attack, Seattle had conducted a blackout practice. When the sirens blared at 10:30 p.m., residents and businesses knew that they had ten minutes to extinguish their lights. Drivers were to pull over and turn off their vehicle lights. After this practice run, protocols were established and shadowed by smaller communities like Grays Harbor.

ON DECEMBER 8, 1941, the day after the Pearl Harbor attack, reports of Japanese aircraft carriers off the Pacific coast put all of the western states on high alert. In Seattle, the blackout alert went into effect at 11:00 p.m., but in downtown, crowds began forming. As they walked the city, many began smashing windows and throwing rocks at offending lights. From this incident, it was quickly realized that crowd control had to be implemented.

Businesses' blackout procedures were then modified, especially for the bars. In Seattle, an ordinance made it illegal for more than five to congregate on any sidewalk, street, alley or place. Driving speeds without lights was reduced to fifteen miles per hour. The sale of liquor was banned during blackout periods. Most of the enforcement was accomplished by volunteer Civil Defense air-raid wardens. They would wear white steel helmets and arm bands as they checked houses and stores in their neighborhoods. Repeat violators would be fined. By October 1943, blackout restrictions were relaxed. Blackout tests, however, still continued for the remainder of the war, but were eventually reduced to Sunday nights only between the hours of 9:30 p.m. and midnight.[4]

HOQUIAM'S FIRST AIR-RAID warning, sounded by the shrill of the mill horns, was Monday night, December 8, 1941. Nightly practice continued over the next few weeks and then it laxed. But what did remain until the war ended, was that all lights had to be out by 10:00 p.m. Only flashlights with blue cellophane over them could be used.[5]

Lee Thomasson, who lived on Cleveland Avenue in the west end of Hoquiam, stated that his block warden, Herb Root, made the nightly stroll around the block during the blackout. If any homeowner violated the ordinance, they would receive a knock on the door with a friendly reminder.

Lee also recalled military trucks passing his home on their way up the hill to Circle Drive. Circle Drive, the highest point of the hill, had spectacular views of Grays Harbor Bay and was the location of the newly erected radar station. Convoys of soldiers also passed through Hoquiam, heading to the beach.

During rationing, bubble gum was one of the hard-to-get items. Lee kept his ear close to his grocery-store connections. When a new supply of bubble gum arrived, he was one of the first kids to put down five cents for the highly-sought commodity.

THE DAY AFTER Labor Day, September 4, 1945, school started and the war was officially over. Hoquiam schools resumed to a pre-war stature. Sports became a leading attraction and the Hoquiam basketball team started a three-year domination. Football was in the spotlight too with Jack Elway having one of the best passing arms in the conference. (Note: Jack was the father to Denver Bronco Quarterback, John Elway.) [6]

BY 1947, traditions for the "Big Game" between Aberdeen and Hoquiam on Thanksgiving Day at the Olympic Stadium had resumed. The week leading up to the game was so festive, it is doubtful that much learning was being done: daily pep rallies, signs being made and displayed, plus early orders of Chrysanthemum corsages for game day was a must.

The corsages were pre-ordered by the girls for $1.00 each. Hoquiam's corsages were white with a red "H" in the middle and red bow. Aberdeen followed the same trend, except their corsage was yellow with a blue "A" in the center and blue bow tied to the stem.

The band and cheer squad from Aberdeen and Hoquiam walked to the opposing team's school, cheering along the way and performing when they reached their destination. The night before Thanksgiving, the Senior Class put on a play for the whole school, and the Saturday after the game, a formal dance was held. [7]

AS THE DECADE wound down, Superintendent Crumpacker announced his retirement. His twenty-five years of service included the difficult years of the Great Depression and World War II. The class of 1949 honored him with a dedication in the *Hesperian*. They thanked him for carrying the school through the Depression, all on a cash basis, which included the 1936 addition of a new gym and classrooms. And for keeping spirits up during WWII.

CHAPTER 9
LEE THOMASSON'S
SCHOOL RECOLLECTIONS
(1945-1958)

SEPTEMBER 4, 1945, several days after the war had ended, Lee Thomasson started the morning kindergarten at Central No. 2. Mrs. Krekow was his teacher. His parent's business, Wheatly Cleaners at 407 Simpson Avenue, was within view from the school.

Lee walked to and from school on his own, ate lunch at the family shop, and took his afternoon nap amidst the shop's noisy machinery. The Central Park playground with a wading pool was a block away and a perfect haven for a five-year old.

CENTRAL NO. 2
(Courtesy of the Polson Museum,
Hoquiam, Wash.2013.046.0040)

1945 CENTRAL NO. 2 KINDERGARTEN CLASS
Lee Thomasson, front row, far right in dark sweater
(Lee H. Thomasson's collection)

With his routine in place, except for the nap, now changed to an afternoon class, Lee started first grade at Central No. 2 in September 1946. When the school board discovered that Lee lived on the wrong side of Cleveland, his parents were summoned. The rule was that students who lived on the right side of Cleveland belonged at Emerson Elementary. Those on the left side belonged at Central No. 2.

Mrs. Thomasson, an expert seamstress, worked long hours as did Lee's father running the business. His parents pleaded their case, but the school board replied, "no exceptions." After arrangements were made with Lee's grandmother, Mrs. Brenneman, Lee transferred to Emerson Elementary. Miss Rosenberg was his teacher.

WHEN LEE returned to the Hoquiam High School compound in 1952 for seventh grade, he was approaching thirteen. Junior high was an eye opener, but not just for Lee, but for all of the kids who were merged from the four elementaries, where they had one class and in most cases one teacher. Now they faced six different classes in one day, each with a new teacher, and three minutes to make the next class.

They all had similar anxieties: "Where is my classroom? My locker? I have to learn a combination? What if I need to use the restroom, how do I do that and get to class in three minutes? Or what if I can't get my locker opened?"

One of Lee's first concerns was what to do in a fire drill. Emerson was one-story with all classroom doors opening to a covered walkway. They could be evacuated in three to four minutes. Junior high was two different buildings, both of them two stories. On Lee's first day, he was lost. Luckily, he hooked up with an upper classman who helped him find all of his classes. Over the next few weeks, he plus the others, settled into a routine, but the social aspects of breaking away from your elementary schoolmates, the school rules, and expanded classes, took a bit longer to maneuver.

JUNIOR HIGH brought fashion awareness to the boys. Principal Morey Wood was known for his brown-leather English Brogue shoes with a built-in heel tap. He wore them almost daily and could be heard coming from a good distance away. These Oxford-type shoes became very popular among the boys. Lee even owned a pair. Another hit was the peg pants with medium to wide legs that tapered and cuffed at the ankles and sat high on the waist. Lee accessorized his with a narrow suede belt.

Junior high was also Lee's first and only encounter of a hacking. Teacher, Frank Barker, had a grip like a blacksmith's vice. Once he grabbed onto Lee's shoulder, there was no way of squirming loose. With that tight grip, he escorted Lee down to the principal's office, then told him to bend over, but not before showing him the wooden paddle peppered with holes. Lee stated that he wasn't sure what was worse: the embarrassment or the pain or the whizzing sound through the holes, but one thing was certain, he would never face that predicament again.

DURING LEE'S junior-high years, he always had a job. In the seventh grade, he delivered the Washingtonian weekly newspaper. The man who oversaw distribution was J. Val Dalby. With every new hire, J. Val drove that person through their route, explaining how each customer liked their paper delivered.

J. Val had a strong work ethic and unique personality, even in the way he dressed: white shirt, tie, apron, plastic green visor, black arm bands up to the elbows, white-ox gloves with fingertips cut off, and a cigar in his mouth.

Lee's route was from Fifth Street south to the railroad tracks. He delivered the paper every Thursday and earned a silver dollar. As time went on, he also learned "stuffing." A newspaper term, where two boys put the first printed section into the second printed section. If you stuffed and delivered you earned two silver dollars a week. Lee signed on. He worked at the Washingtonian for two years. As circulation was winding down, the papers were no longer delivered. Instead, they were mailed. He earned his two silver coins by stuffing and delivering a canvas bag of newspapers to the post office.

In addition to his newspaper job, Lee, now fourteen, worked for Chuck Morsetti, owner of West End Grocery. He stocked shelves, cleaned the butcher shop, and tended to the produce, plus assisted with deliveries.

One of Lee's Silver Dollars
(Lee H. Thomasson's collection)

During high school, he hired on with Coast Oyster, near Hogan's Corner at Ocean Shores. This job required a work permit and social security card. The crew worked with the tides and every day had a different starting time, but Lee never missed school. In his freshman and sophomore years, he was the stadium concession vendor at all of the home games, walking the grandstands and yelling, "peanuts, popcorn, and candy bars." The items were provided by the school concession stand. He earned a percentage of every piece he sold and usually walked away with three to four dollars.

In 1956, his parents divorced. With his savings, he helped his mother buy Adell's Flowers in Aberdeen. He, his brother, and mother relocated to Aberdeen where he worked as a florist and drove the delivery truck. He continued at Hoquiam High School and graduated in 1958.

GROWING UP IN THE '50s
Story by: Lee H. Thomasson
Hoquiam High School Class of 1958

LEE THOMASSON (17) 1958
During Pioneer Days, the high school
boys were allowed to grow beards for a contest.

GROWING UP IN THE *'50s* was a wonderful era. It was the sounds of rock 'n' roll, the Chevy 'split' manifolds and dual Smitty Glasspack mufflers barking as the car went through the gears. We had Jack's Drive-In, the Short Stop Drive-In and the Tip Top Drive-In for hang outs. Hamburgers were 25 cents and so were the shakes. Twenty-five cents would buy a movie at the 7th Street Theater and a gallon of gas at Bingers. For 10 cents you could get a Green River drink at the Oriole Café in Hoquiam. There was pool at Popeyes' as well as wonderful greasy hamburgers for 25 cents.

GROWING UP IN THE '50s (Continued)

SPORTS WERE TAKEN seriously and Hoquiam's mascot, Sammy Blackmore, would tell you the dates and location of every game and let you rub his "lucky" rabbit's foot. The annual Thanksgiving Day game between Hoquiam and Aberdeen was broadcast by Bob Hoonan and every house had the game on at either KBKW or KXRO. Turkey was not eaten until the game was over.

SUMMERS WERE WARM and we all went to Aberdeen Lake to swim and to meet girls or for the other half, boys. Several times in the '50s, the lakes were closed due to polio outbreaks. The '50s also saw the end of polio. Elizabeth Gorley, Hoquiam's school nurse, would track you down to give you a polio shot. She missed no one!

On summer nights, a drag race could be found on the Moon Island Road. Top cars went to Aberdeen and drag raced on the Westport Highway. We drank beer when we could get it and everyone smoked and thought they looked 'adult.'

THE TIMES WEREN'T perfect but we never locked our doors to our cars or homes. Everyone knew the local cops. 'Sooty' Cyrs was Hoquiam's motorcycle cop. Captain John Schneider smoked cigars all night long in his HPD patrol car and you could smell him a block away on a warm summer night.

The times we grew up in are still kept alive and well by both movies and television. The music we played for 5 cents at Popeyes' is still being played on the radio stations. Who can forget driving to a dance at Harm's Hall in Westport and listening to Patsy Cline singing "Walking After Midnight" on our AM radios?

We all have our memories and our stories about the '50s. The Hoquiam Class of 1958 was a product of the '50s and we still are.

Lee H. Thomasson, H.H.S Class of 1958

LEE'S CAR
1950 Ford—Lipstick Red
(Courtesy of Lee H. Thomasson's collection)

ANOTHER REMEMBRANCE of the 1950s, was Ed Bowers' Redwood tree that shined bright at Christmas, high on the hill on Sunset Drive. Lee could see it from his front yard.

Planted from a seedling in the 1940s, it grew to be almost twenty-five feet high. Once it reached a significant height, Mr. Bowers, owner of Interstate Asphalt, had a pulley system devised with Christmas lights. Music was later added. The tree could be viewed from almost every street on the western end of Hoquiam. It became such a joy to the families below, that every year kids would venture up to the hill to see and hear the tree up close. Others would stand in their yards and sing along.

Mr. Bowers struck an agreement with his neighbor, Hilland Hubble, that he'd replace Mr. Hubble's roof every fifteen years or so from the damage that the tree's needles had caused. Mr. Bowers also had an arrangement with the National Weather Service. If a storm was on its way, they'd contact him and he'd immediately lower the lights until it passed.

Mr. Bowers' generosity of time and money demonstrated an allegiance to his community. The Seventh Street Theater still stands today because of his involvement.

AFTER HIGH SCHOOL, Lee secured a position at KBKW Radio where he met his first wife, Deana Colton. They had two children and were married forty-three years until her passing in 2004.

In 1963, he graduated from Grays Harbor College, then worked in the sign business for three years. In 1966, he was hired by Pacific Northwest Bell telephone and went on to become a communication worker for thirty-five years, until his retirement in 2001 from Qwest Communications. He later married Hoquiam High School classmate Joyce Nicholson (née Richardson).

LEE WAS ALWAYS involved with the community. He became a scoutmaster, a board of director member for the Twin Harbors Council, an officer for the Communication Workers of America, a member of the Telephone Pioneers, a Hoquiam Grizzly Alumni Board member, a fifty-year member of the Aberdeen Elks, and a thirty-year member of the Sons of Norway. He also received awards: the Scouting District Award, the Silver Beaver, and the 2022 Polson Museum Pioneer of the Year.

He was the past president and a current member of the Alexander Hamilton Chapter of S.A.R. (Sons of the American Revolution) and of Descendants of Washington's Army at Valley Forge. His wife Joyce is a member of D.A.R. (Daughters of the American Revolution). When dressed in their Revolutionary attire, they attend community events as well as local elementary schools to instill patriotism and teach the history of America.

In 2008, they organized the Class of 1958's fiftieth Hoquiam High School Reunion. Lee and Joyce produced a video about the class that covered the years 1940 through present. It was so well received that the classmates placed orders for copies. Lee and Joyce donated the proceeds to the Grays Harbor College scholarship fund in memory of the Class of 1958's favorite teacher, David Waller.

(Courtesy of Lee Thomasson's collection)

CHAPTER 10
1950s ELEMENTARY SCHOOLS
CENTRAL NO. 3

WITH THE RETURN of the soldiers from war, came the "baby boom." During the 1950's, many of Hoquiam's aging schools needed renovation or demolition to prepare for the influx of this new population. Gone were the turn-of-the-century opulent buildings, they were now being replaced with one-story, modernized structures that were faster to build.

IN 1951, THE HOQUIAM School Board directors developed a long-range plan for the building needs of all of the schools in their district. The first in line was a new and larger Central Elementary, Central No. 3, for the students living in the central portion of town. Once Central No. 3 was completed Central No. 2 was to be converted for Junior and Senior High school use.

CENTRAL NO. 3 ELEMENTARY SCHOOL
(Replaced Central No. 2)
(Courtesy of Jones Photo Historical Collection 29602_1)

CENTRAL NO. 3, built in 1953, extended almost the entire block between Third and Fourth Streets and J Street and Simpson with various buildings. The 32,371 square-foot main structure, with a cost of half a million dollars, encompassed twelve classrooms, a kindergarten, a library, nurse's headquarters, and administration offices, plus a large multi-purpose/recreation area and a combined gymnasium and auditorium.

The auditorium's removable seats would accommodate up to six hundred people. When not in use, the seats would be stored under the stage. The gymnasium, not planned for spectator sports, was planned to hold folding bleachers. Their school colors were blue and white and team name, the Bears.

Mrs. Krekow was teaching kindergarten at Central No. 2 in the 1940s. With the completion of Central No. 3, her kindergarten classes were moved to the new school. Central No. 3 kindergarten was designed as a separate unit with its own lavatory and fenced play area.

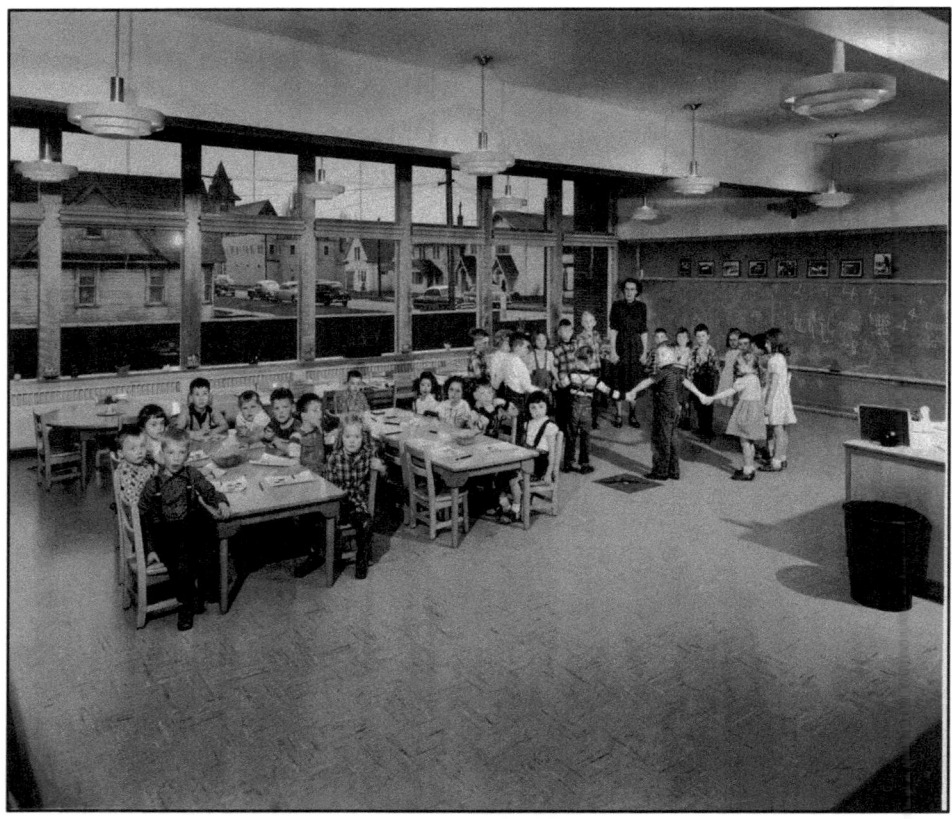

CENTRAL NO. 3 KINDERGARTEN, 1954
(Mrs. Edna Krekow's Kindergarten class)
(Courtesy of Jones Photo Historical Collection 28180_1)

Grades one through three also had designated classroom bathrooms. The intermediate classes, four through six, had one large auxiliary restroom for girls, painted pink. The one for boys was painted blue.

All of the classrooms were at the highest level of innovation. Each had long work cabinets with low counters equipped with a sink and storage space. Convector radiators heated all rooms, except for kindergarten, it had radiant heat in the floors. Placement of wood light baffles under the monitor windows on the north side of the classrooms diffused light. Each room was also designed with north lighting to provide maximum daylight and to ensure that the direct summer sun rays would not reach the window until after five p.m. [1]

CENTRAL NO. 3 ELEMENTARY SCHOOL CLASSROOM
(Mrs. Thelma Love's Second-Grade class)
(Courtesy of Jones Photo Historical Collection 28179_1)

THE ADMINISTRATIVE OFFICES AT Central No. 3 included a main reception room for the offices of Superintendent Bohrnsen, Assistant Superintendent Frank Bowen, and Central No. 3 Principal Strandwold. This building also included a meeting room for the school district board, a teachers' room, a work room for special activities, and the nurse's quarters, which included a three-bed ward and an ear and eye examination station.

**CENTRAL NO. 3
ADMINISTRATIVE OFFICES**
(Courtesy of Larry R. Jones collection)

CHAPTER 11
PARENT-TEACHER ASSOCIATION "ELEMENTARY" YEARBOOK

EMERSON SCHOOL AND PARENT-TEACHER ASSOCIATION YEARBOOK
Rules, Regulations, and Guidelines
1961-1962
(Courtesy of Larry R. Jones' collection)

EMERSON'S MOTTO: Work together—learn together to gain qualified leaders for tomorrow.

ALL OF HOQUIAM'S elementary schools would have followed similar guidelines outlined in Emerson Grade School's Parent - Teacher Association Yearbook.

P.T.A meetings, from 8:00 to 9:00 p.m., were scheduled for the second Monday of each month. A half-hour social time was carved out after. P.T.A dues were $.75 per person or $1.50 per couple. Everyone was welcome to attend, but only the paid members were allowed to vote. Voting included proposed events, school changes, committees, and even the fifth-grade Song Queen tryouts, where the PTA mothers and teachers casted their votes.

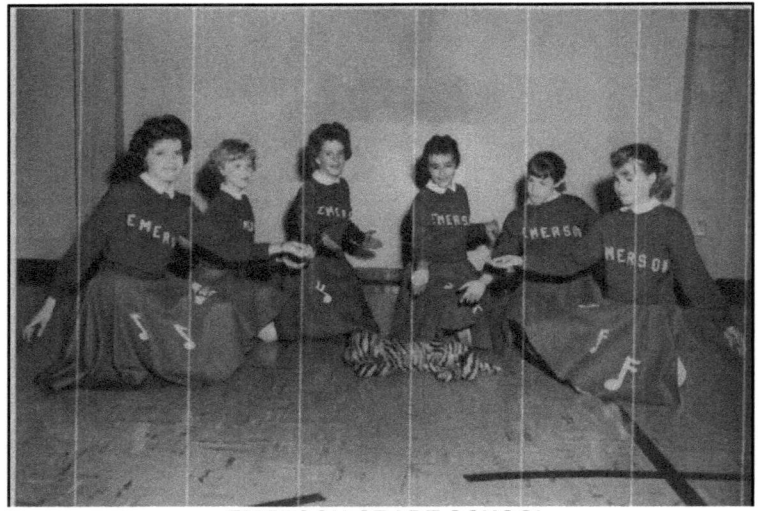

**EMERSON GRADE SCHOOL
1962 SONG QUEENS
"TIGER" MASCOT**
(Courtesy of Larry R. Jones' collection)

Their school colors were green and white and team name, the Tigers.

SCHOOL CALENDAR 1961-1962:

- Pre-school planning conference for all teachers.   Aug. 31 – Sept 1, 1961
- Opening of school   September 8, 1961
- End of first quarter   November 3, 1961
- Thanksgiving vacation   November 23-26, 1961
- Christmas vacation   Dec. 23 - Jan. 2, 1962
- End of first semester   January 19, 1962
- Washington's Birthday   February 22, 1962
- End of third quarter   March 3, 1962
- Spring vacation   April 14-22, 1962
- Memorial Day   May 30, 1962
- End of school   June 5, 1962
- Summer workshop for all teachers   June 6-8, 1962

Absences:

Absent or tardy from school required an acceptable excuse to the teacher the day of return. Excuses were only deemed valid in the case of personal illness or death in the family.

Conferences:
If you wished to confer with the teacher, this had to be scheduled by appointment before or after school or at noon time. Principal Krekow was available throughout most days.

Music:
Violin lessons were provided by Mr. Robbins. Band lessons under the direction of Mr. Mason.

Parents/Parties:
Please do not send pre-school children to school to visit. Parties and/or special treats had to be pre-arranged.

Enrollment Age:
For kindergarten, the child had to be five-years-old on or before November 1st. Those who would be six on or before November 1st, could enter first grade.

National Assemblies:

Trained Animal Show	Wednesday, September 20, 1961	9:00 a.m.
Marionettes	Monday, December 4, 1961	9:00 a.m.
Royal Scotsman	Monday, January 29, 1962	9:00 a.m.
Nature Film	Tuesday, February 20, 1962	9:00 a.m.
Organist	Monday, March 19, 1962	9:00 a.m.
Big Game Hunter	Wednesday, April 11, 1962	9:00 a.m.

SCHOOL-GROUND RULES:

Entrance:
a. Kindergarten—had its own entrance.
b. Primary grades—west end, rear door. Grades 4,5,6 nearest to classroom.
c. Only those accompanied by parents could use the front or porch entrances.

Lavatories:
a. No playing around the lavatories or running in the pass-way behind the lavatories.
b. Always flush the toilet and put towels in the basket.
c. Report important lavatory problems to your teacher.

Porch:
a. No bouncing balls against the walls
b. Inflated balls were the only ones permitted in the porch area.
c. Roller skating was only permitted after 4 o'clock.
d. While skating, no cracking the whip or sweeps.
e. No scooters, tricycles, bicycles or wagons were permitted on the porch at any time.

Playground:
a. No fighting on grounds or on the way home.
b. No throwing of stones or snowballs.
c. Keeping off of the grandstand. Children could sit on the first and second steps.
d. No playing under the grandstand.
e. Keeping away from the janitor's room, unless on an errand.
f. Staying away from the High School equipment.
g. Staying off the roof and keeping off the lawn at all times.

Playground Equipment:
a. Bars:
 – Upper-grade children could use the "monkey bars" in the morning.
 – Primary children could use them in the afternoon.
 – Noon time use of the bars was a free period for those who ate in the cafeteria or brought cold lunches.
 – When on the bars, the children had to move in the same direction.
 – No walking or sitting on the bars.
b. Tether Balls:
 – Balls by the grandstand were for the primary grades.
 – Balls on the east end were for the upper grades.
c. Merry-Go-Round
 – Were for the primary students only.

Lunch:
a. Children living within a five-block radius could not bring a cold lunch unless special permission was granted.
b. Hot lunch $1.50 per week or 33 cents for a single lunch.

c. Any discourteous children would be barred from the lunch room.
d. Milk for cold lunches was 15 cents a ticket, good for three glasses.

<u>Miscellaneous</u>:
a. Children were not to come to school before 8:30 a.m. nor return from lunch before 12:45 p.m., except for those who ate in the cafeteria or brought cold lunches. The hot-lunch children were not allowed to leave the school grounds at noon without a note from home.

THE NATIONAL ASSEMBLIES were a big hit with the kids, especially the "trained animal show," which one time featured a black bear. When a student was called to the stage to help with a stunt, he started throwing boxing punches toward the bear. The six-grader was immediately escorted back to his seat.

MOTHERS VOLUNTEERED as "room mothers," for special parties or events. They were also active committee members for venues, such as the yearly school carnival and art show.

IN ADDITION TO teaching, teachers were assigned additional tasks:

a. <u>Lunch Duty</u>:
   - Primary students (Grades 1-3) ate first. The teacher on duty started at 11:25 a.m. The children remained in the lunch room until 11:50 a.m. In bad weather, this same teacher would supervise the children until the hall supervisor came on duty at 12:30 p.m.
   - Upper students (Grades 4-6) assembled into the lunch room at 11:55 a.m. with a new teacher supervisor, who was also responsible for maintenance of a clean playground and hallway.

b. <u>Hall and Playground</u>. A teacher was on duty from 8:30 a.m. to 8:55 a.m. and from 12:20 p.m. to 12:40 p.m. In bad weather, several fifth and sixth graders might be asked to assist with the primary students.

c. <u>Recess</u>: One primary and one upper-grade teacher were on duty at all times. In bad weather, each room played in designated areas. Recess times: 10:15 to 10:30 a.m., 12:40 to 12:55 p.m., and 2:00 to 2:15 p.m.

d. <u>Teacher's Room</u>: The week that a teacher was on lunch duty, he or she was also responsible for keeping the teacher's room neat.

e. <u>School buses</u>: Teachers were assigned to organize lines and signal the driver to depart.

CHILDREN RIDING THE school buses were under direct supervision of the driver. Any bus problems were to be directed to the driver or to the assistant superintendent. Emerson's two afternoon buses left between 3:20 to 3:40 p.m. Children would line up outside. If the weather was bad, they'd wait in the hall. The buses would not depart until the teacher signaled the driver that all children were aboard.

Bus rules and regulations were prepared by the State Superintendent of Public Instruction with the advice of the Chief of the State Patrol and Director of Highways. These applied to all school buses operating in the state:

a. The driver was fully in charge.
b. Students had to obey the driver, promptly and willingly.
c. No student was to extend his head, hands, or arms out of the windows.
d. Students were to remain in their seats while the bus was in motion and could not get on or off until the bus came to a full stop.
e. Students could <u>only</u> cross the highway in front of the bus.
f. No student should sit in the driver's seat, nor to the left or right of the driver.
g. Any student disobeying the driver, could be restrained from riding the bus.

FIRE DRILLS
a. Fire drills, held twice monthly, were assisted by the custodian. It required approximately 45 seconds for the students to empty the building.

SCHOOL-BOY PATROL
a) Was an organization of fifth-grade boys commissioned by the State Patrol.
b) They worked directly under the supervision of the City Police Department and the school principal.
c) They were authorized to take charge of private and public vehicle traffic.
d) When on duty, the children were to follow their command when crossing the street at Emerson Avenue and/or the corner of Emerson and Adams.

THE TEACHERS OF EMERSON'S 1961-1962 SCHOOL TERM:

Krekow, Waldemar G.	Principal
Blevins, Corine B.	First-grade teacher
Drake, Shirley	Fourth-grade teacher
Elmore, Margaret R.	Second-grade teacher
Haunreiter, Katherine	Remedial
Holevas, Marilyn F.	Third-grade teacher
Jones, Larry R.	Sixth-grade teacher
Kogin, Diane M.	First-grade teacher
Lewis, Idabel F.	Sixth-grade teacher
Maesner, Virginia R.	Fourth-grade teacher
Mann, Lillian S.	Fifth-grade teacher
Rosenberg, Frances F.	First-grade teacher
Sandstedt, Darlene L.	Second-grade teacher
Warjonen, Chetta T.	Third-grade teacher
Wilcox, Sally M.	Kindergarten

ADMINISTRATION

Bohrnsen, William F.	Superintendent
Cook, Eugene H.	Assistant Superintendent
Roy, Ester	Secretary
Kilcup, Anne C.	Secretary

SPECIAL

Eadie, Florence	School Nurse
Lovgren, Oscar	Truancy Officer

CAFETERIA WORKERS:

Riutta, Mary	Cook
Owens, Edith	Helper

CUSTODIANS:

Sandgren, Sylvan	Custodian
Sandgren, Echo	Helper

CHAPTER 12
EMERSON GRADE SCHOOL

EMERSON GRADE SCHOOL (Built 1922)
(Courtesy of the Polson Museum archives)

AS THE WEST END of town grew, the need for a new school became apparent. Unlike the other elementary schools named after a governor or president, Emerson Elementary, built in 1922, was named after one of Hoquiam's founding fathers, George H. Emerson, and located on the cross streets of Emerson Avenue and Adams. Instead of a large two-or-three-story brick and mortar structure, the majority of the school was single story with shingle siding. Miss Nell Allen was the school's first principal.

PICTURED BELOW is the 1929-1930 second and third-grade students of Emerson Elementary.

EMERSON GRADE SCHOOL
SECOND AND THIRD GRADE CLASS
1929-1930
(Authors' collection)

Back row (L to R): Dale Pendergraft, Morice Harmon, Roy Benson, Harold Worthley, Fred Compton, Bob Ryan, Vinko Matulich, Fred Van Ess, Fred McFedy, Chuck Johnson, Carolyn Abramson, Charlotte Swan, Mary Walker, Marjory Kilcup, Anne Brandvick, Charlotte Portman, **Gladys May**, [v] Dorene Worthley, Faye Fisher, Zena Bublitz, Evelyn Erickson, Mary Beth Root, Margaret Powers, Mary Kilcup.

Front row: (L to R): Llewellyn Luce, Chet Ekman, Walter Swanson, Bill Wyckoff, David English, William Giles, Jim Elwin, Eleanor Espedal, Edith Hendrickson, Avanel Pickering, Beatrice Watson, Ruth Walker, Phyllis Keegan, Shirley Bunch, Juanita Doolittle, Betty Ostergard, Ruth Parsons.

---

[v] Gladys May, authors' cousin and niece to Lester Hanson.

EMERSON GRADE SCHOOL TEACHERS (Circa 1930s)
(Courtesy of the Polson Museum, Hoquiam, Wash., 2011.023.0006)
TEACHERS (L to R): Ruth Birks, Gladys Prouty, Louise H. Meyer, Katherine Sharpe, Winona Crumb, Miss Watts, **Miss Nell B. Allen**[w], and **Miss Rosenberg**.

MESSAGE TO THE PARENT printed on the 1930 report cards:

We have endeavored to give you as much definite and valuable information in the report as possible. The credit made in a subject is not the only important thing in a pupil's school career. His attitude, interests, spirit, and conduct are very important. We are, therefore, including these in this report. The natural incentives to do good work are interest, pride in work, the sense of duty, competition, the winning of approval, and the desire to prepare for a useful and happy life. The school aims to rely on these, appealing to the more artificial motives when necessary.

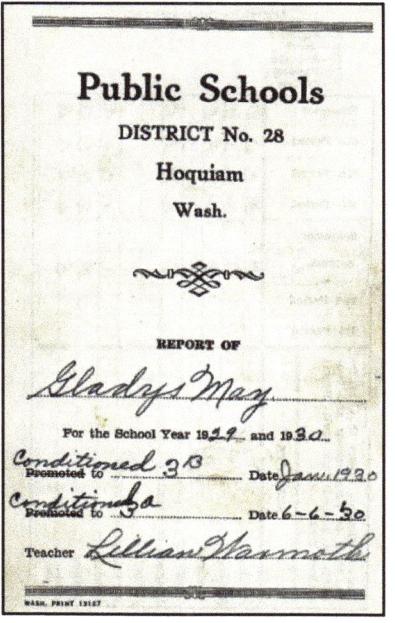

---

[w] Nell Allen (pictured) was Emerson's first principal (1922-1941). Her replacement was Mr. Krekow.

**MISS DEL DUCCA'S
FOURTH GRADE CLASS (1931)**
(Authors' collection)
(L to R): Vinko Matulich, Margaret Powers, Dale Pendergraft, Zena Bublitz, Fred Van Ess, and Gladys May

**EMERSON BASKETBALL
TEAM, 1932**
(Courtesy of the Polson Museum, Hoquiam, Wash., 1998.100.0001)

(L to R): Sam English, Lemuel Elway, Herber Haley, Gerald Blagen, Eugene Arwin, Harlan Arwin, Louis Welch, Bob Davies, Sam Satow, Harry Elway.

Excerpt from newspaper article.

See full article in **Reference** section at the back of this book:

Pennies contributed by school children in **HOQUIAM** and other American communities made possible the re-conditioning of the historic frigate...

Gladys May's Emerson Grade School Sixth-grade Class

1933 Field trip to Old *Ironsides* at Port Dock

(Authors' collection)

1935 EMERSON GRADE SCHOOL RELAY TEAM
Relay racers run shirtless
(Courtesy of the Polson Museum, Hoquiam, Wash. 2023.039.0002)

Note on picture: **We made a new county relay mark 59.2**

EMERSON FIELD WAS built behind the Emerson School playground. It housed an enclosed grandstand and two open-aired bleachers for viewing football and track and field events, plus other venues such as the first Loggers' Playday in 1964. From the 1920s through the late 1930s, it was the home of the annual Aberdeen vs. Hoquiam Thanksgiving games. It was also used for practice and hosting Emerson Grade School sporting events.

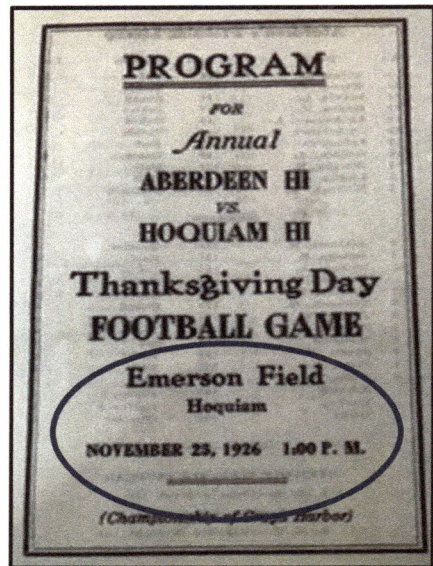

1926 AND 1928 PROGRAMS
(Authors' collection)

EMERSON FIELD 1936
ABERDEEN – HOQUIAM THANKSGIVING GAME
(Courtesy of the Polson Museum, Hoquiam, Wash., 1990.058.0001)

EMERSON ELEMENTARY

1943-1944 EMERSON GRADE SCHOOL TRACK TEAM
(Courtesy of the Polson Museum, Hoquiam, Wash.2023.039.015)

1944 EMERSON GRADE SCHOOL CITY TRACK CHAMPS
(Courtesy of the Polson Museum, Hoquiam, Wash. 2023.039.0018)

This is during WWII. The coach in his Navy uniform and many of the boys are wearing sailor hats.

**1946 MISS ROSENBERG'S FIRST-GRADE CLASS
EMERSON GRADE SCHOOL**
Front Row: **third from the left: Lee Thomasson**
(Courtesy of Lee H. Thomasson's collection)

MISS ROSENBERG was one of Lee's favorite teachers. He attributes his love of reading to her. She had a fondness to him as well. The summer after he had graduated from her first-grade class, she sent him a postcard from Minnesota.

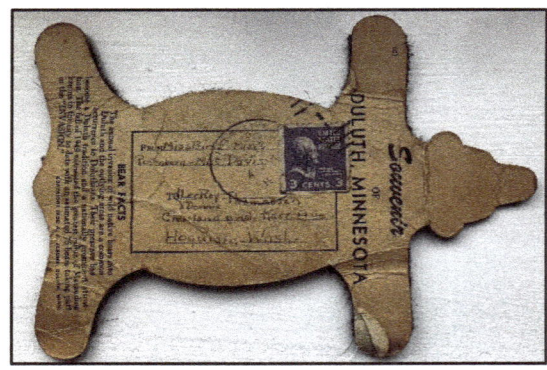

FUZZY BEAR POSTCARD
From Miss Rosenberg
(Courtesy of Lee H. Thomasson's collection)

A FAVORITE TEACHER

ELEMENTARY SCHOOL teachers, especially those who taught first grade, appear to be the most remembered. This was the period when children were learning their alphabet and forming them into words.

One of the most beloved teachers at Emerson Grade School was Frances Rosenberg. A graduate of Aberdeen High School, she returned to Grays Harbor after college to teach school.

Known as "Rosie" to her friends, she taught for more than forty years at Emerson Elementary. She is mentioned by students at different spans of time, and all with the same fond sentiment.

For sixty years, she and teacher, Ruth Birks, shared a house on Emerson Avenue, down a block from the school. Through the 1950s, teacher Madeline Davis lived there too.

Many times, students who she had taught years prior would catch her walking and accompany her on the short walk to her home. She was always pleased to see them and to hear about their lives. After twelve years, her first students had graduated high school. She sent all of them a congratulations card and continued this ritual for years to come.[1]

FRANCES ROSENBERG
1920 Aberdeen Yearbook

IN THE THIRD grade, Lee was home with the Chickenpox. He missed the Valentine Party, so his classmates sent him get-well cards.

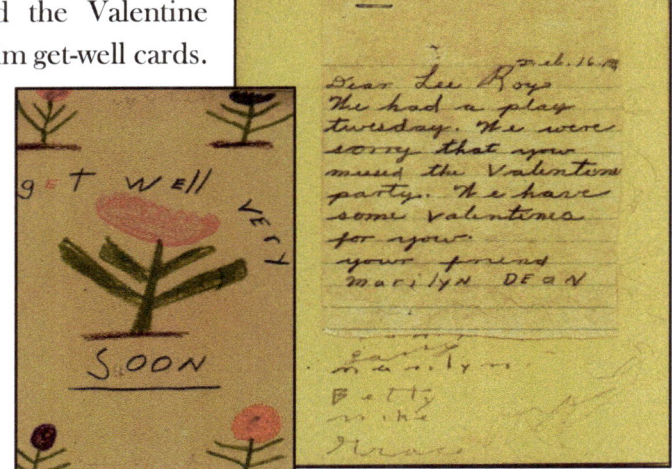

GET WELL CARD
From classmates
(Courtesy of Lee H. Thomasson's collection)

EMERSON GRADE SCHOOL THIRD-GRADE CLASS
Teacher: ILENE WOOD KLEIN
(Courtesy of Lee H. Thomasson's collection)

IN THE LATE 1940s at Emerson Grade School, civil-defense dog tags were offered to the children for 25 cents. The tags contained the student's name, address, faith and other pertinent information. It was to be used to identify the child in case of a nuclear attack.

LEE THOMASSON'S DOG TAG
(Courtesy of Lee H. Thomasson's collection)

THERE WERE SEVERAL people at Emerson who Lee considered special. They weren't teachers, but were the staff who kept the school running. One was Floyd Casselman, known as Cassie, Emerson's custodian.

Cassie always wore white pinstriped bib overalls and rode a bike to and from school. Whenever the teacher needed a note taken to him, Lee jumped at the chance to go to his office, which was the furnace room at the far east end of the school. It had a table, chair, clock and a radio and was next to a large covered area piled high with green-chain slabs from the local sawmill. The slabs were rough-cut wood with sawdust on them and were wet and heavy.

Keeping the furnace running was Cassie's main job. The hot water was pumped to all of the rooms to keep them warm. Cassie would burn all of the school trash in the furnace. He also kept a stack of the rough-cut wood in his office to dry before tossing it into the firebox. Then would retrieve more. He had an assortment of tools and did small repairs too, plus cleaned the school. He was never sitting. In later years, people with metal detectors dug through the old furnace ashes looking for coins.

KATE DEHAVEN, the head cook at Emerson, was one of the nicest people at the school. She prepared a wonderful menu geared for the kids and her meals were always delicious. Lee often asked her to cook something that he liked and she always did. His mother sent her flowers several times to thank her.

ONE MEMORABLE DAY at Emerson was during a morning recess in 1949. Lee was in the third grade. It was a nice day, so he and several other boys headed to the baseball field. As they were tossing the ball, the ground began rolling. Suddenly, they heard snapping from the grandstand that sounded like rifle shots. They stared in disbelief as the grandstand swayed back and forth as nails shot out.

The kids had been drilled on proper earthquake protocol: to stay away from tall poles and trees and sit in an area away from any structures. Lee and his friends quickly sat down. But many of the older kids didn't, instead, they raced to the grandstand to catch a ride.

EMERSON GRANDSTAND
(Courtesy of the Polson Museum, Hoquiam, Wash.1990.017.006)

1922 "ORIGINAL" EMERSON GRADE SCHOOL
(Authors' collection)

ON MARCH 8, 1955, the Hoquiam School Board presented a $600,000 bond to the voters for necessary repairs and updates for all of the public schools in District 28.

The Emerson Grade School changes included the removal of the entire west wing after engineers had determined that it wasn't feasible to continue with maintenance. The old section that remained was renovated with new wiring and lighting, plus a restructure: the old administrative area became the library, the old furnace room was reconstructed into the remedial room, and the old woodshed into a classroom. The breezeway was enclosed and the lavatories were modernized and refinished.

The new west wing added six primary classrooms, a multi-purpose room with a cafeteria kitchen, an administrative area, and a new heating plant. It followed the flat-roof design of the newly built Central Elementary. A kindergarten classroom was also created.

EMERSON GRADE SCHOOL
New west wing after 1956 updates
The old section is attached to the "right"
(Courtesy of Larry R. Jones' collection)

ALMOST EVERYONE can recall their first day of school. Each experience unique, yet threaded with the common fear of new environments and people. Diane's stories encapsulate those early school years from a child's view.

KINDERGARTEN, 1959-1960
Emerson Grade School, Hoquiam, WA
Story by: Diane Taylor

THE MORNING OF September 8, 1959, my mother and I walked hand-in-hand to Emerson Grade School to attend my first kindergarten class. Back then, only half-day kindergarten classes existed. I was in Mrs. Wilcox's morning class. Mrs. Wilcox was a pretty brunette with a bubbly personality who always wore red-leather shoes.

That first day of kindergarten was quite shocking when I learned that my own mother wanted to leave me with a bunch of kids I didn't know and at a place I was unfamiliar with. I cried, fussed, and pleaded with my mother as she let go of my hand. During this drastic moment, I couldn't help but think about my life at home with just mommy and me: my storybooks, my Tickle Bee game, and my favorite Disney show, the Mouseketeer Club. What else did I need besides all that?

Mrs. Wilcox took my hand and led me to one of the long tables filled with children coloring, assembling puzzles, and stacking building blocks. As I sat, she reassured me that I'd be alright and grow to like it here.

The morning whizzed by as Mrs. Wilcox entertained eighteen plus of us with her character voice of Lamb Chop, a hand puppet, telling us fun stories with sing-alongs. My favorite play along was going on a bear hunt with Mrs. Wilcox. As she told the story, we would join in with chilling sounds while going through the deep forest. We were so excited with the bear hunt that we didn't notice the two sixth graders standing before us until they announced snacks! Milk and animal crackers were deliciously devoured just at the right time, then we took a nap.

Afterwards, we lined our chairs, back-to-back, for musical chairs while Mrs. Wilcox turned on the record player to play the tune: "Pop Goes the Weasel." The winner got to choose the next games. "London Bridges" and "I'm a Little Teapot," were some that we all sang and played.

KINDERGARTEN, 1959-1960 (Continued)
Emerson Grade School, Hoquiam, WA
Story by: Diane Taylor

With the weather outside now warm, we lined up single-file and headed to the playground for another game and song: "Old MacDonald Had a Farm." Before I knew it, I was getting my coat to leave when I saw all of the mothers, including mine, waiting outside to pick us up.

From then on, I enjoyed every day spent in Mrs. Wilcox's class. Before the Christmas break, our mothers joined our class to make a clay mold with OUR HANDPRINT, dated 1959.

Mrs. Wilcox radiated with humor, wit, and patience, and to this day, she remains one of my favorite teachers.

MRS. WILCOX'S KINDERGARTEN CLASS (1959-1960)
Diane, back row, sixth from left
(Authors' collection)

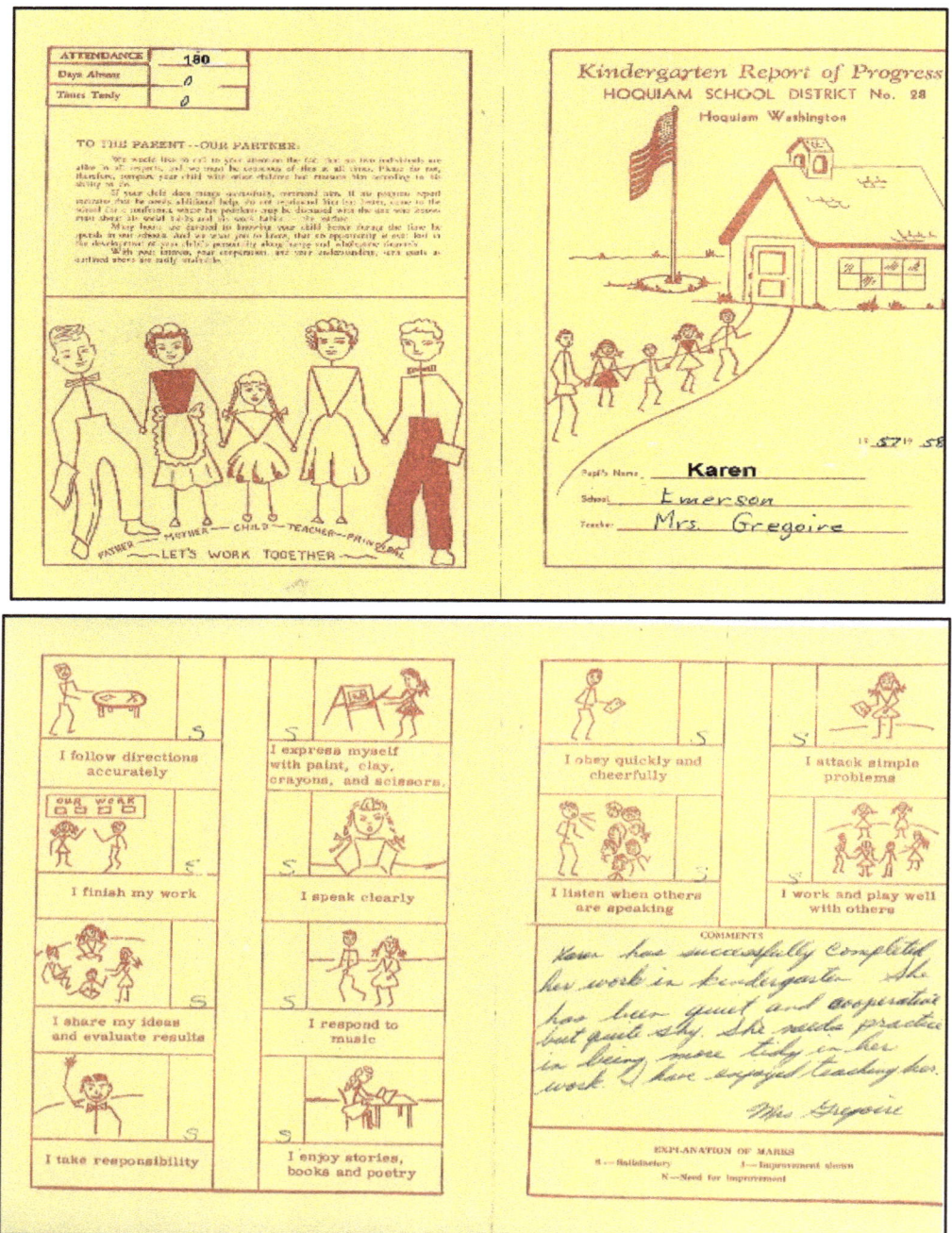

MRS. GREGOIRE'S KINDERGARTEN CLASS
Karen's Report Card
(1957-1958)
(Authors' collection)

IN 1959, THE Emerson Grade School children, who attended the morning kindergarten class, continued with the same classmates through the third grade. Their first-grade teacher was Miss Rosenberg. The same format followed with the afternoon kindergarteners who were assigned to Mrs. Blevins' first-grade class.

FIRST GRADE, 1960-1961
Emerson Grade School
Hoquiam, Washington
Story by: Diane Taylor

MISS ROSENBERG
(Authors' collection)

MISS ROSENBERG WAS the favorite teacher of my older brother and sister. She became one of my favorites as well. She began her teaching career at Emerson Elementary in the 1930's and had mastered a mix of humor, firmness, and kindness in her teaching. Many times, she'd start the day with a joke, and at recess playtime, tell us to be back on time, but to also have fun, be nice, and share alike.

On our first day of class, she introduced her rules and conduct expectations and had us repeat them. Then called upon various students to ensure they were listening, then had the entire class repeat them again.

FIRST GRADE, 1960-1961 (CONTINUED)

The alphabet determined our seating order, and with my surname starting with "T," I was always placed at the back. This could be advantageous, but also a curse when she realized that I wasn't raising my hand to answer, and for that day, she seemed to make it her mission to call on me. Sometimes, more than once!

While we did lessons, she'd hold her long ruler and stroll up and down each row, looking over our shoulders. She never used the ruler as a weapon, but instead as a pointing tool. It was always a relief when she passed by your desk, but a moment of terror when she stopped and down came that ruler tapping on your paper, followed by a whisper on what to correct.

She taught us the history of America and the importance of patriotism. Every morning, we'd stand, face the flag, and with our hand across our heart, pledge our allegiance to the flag. Sometimes after, we'd sing "My Country, Tis' of Thee."

It was in her class where we first learned the alphabet and to read. As she stood at the blackboard, she'd pronounce each letter as she was drawing it out in chalk, large enough for everyone to see. We'd do the same on our wide-lined paper until it filled the page. It was especially fun when we started to form words, like "cat" and "dog." And what a thrill when we had progressed to the colorful "Dick and Jane" books with their dog "Spot." She even allowed us to take the books home for reading practice.

Learning arithmetic, we used our crayons for adding and subtracting. We'd recite the alphabet daily and take turns at the chalkboard writing the letters in front of the class. We'd get homework, sometimes individual assignments to take home too. And how exciting when we'd receive a "gold" star on our paper.

We also did afternoon art: finger painting and water coloring. The classroom had a large sink in the back for cleanup. For special holidays, such as Christmas, we'd make red-and-green construction-paper links that we'd stream around the Christmas Tree.

At the end of the year, we exchanged our individual class pictures and pasted them into our first-grade remembrance book. Sadly, we had to say goodbye to Miss Rosenberg, but through the years she was always a strong remembrance in our hearts.

DIANE
First grade,
Miss Rosenberg

KAREN
First Grade
Miss Rosenberg

DOUG
First Grade
Miss Rosenberg

MISS ROSENBERG'S FIRST-GRADE CLASS
Our brother **Doug**, front row, **second from left**, cowboy shirt.
His best friend, **Danny Kristrom**, front row, **far right.**
(Authors' collection)

THIRD GRADE WAS a turning point for me (Karen). I was no longer in the new wing of the school. My third-grade class was in the tail end of the "L" shaped old structure. A long cold hallway with high windows, which used to be an open breezeway, was lined with hooks to hang our coats before entering the classroom.

Mrs. Holevas, my third-grade teacher, was another one of my favorites. She didn't pace the classroom holding a ruler like my older second-grade teacher, who whacked my knuckles, more than once, with her wooden stick. All because I was holding my pencil incorrectly during penmanship.

Mrs. Holevas taught with kindness. She was approachable and allowed questions while doing classroom assignments.

MRS. HOLEVAS
Karen's third-grade teacher
(Authors' collection)

Diane's third-grade experience shows a different flavor, proving that every situation was unique:

> THIRD GRADE, 1962-1963
> Emerson Grade School
> Hoquiam, Washington
> Story by: Diane Taylor
>
> MRS. WARJONEN taught with firmness and discipline. She'd walk up and down the rows with her ruler in hand as she dictated lessons and observed. If anyone became unruly, she'd summon Principal Krekow, who would appear with his wooden paddle. We could hear every smack, which set a somber mood for the rest of the day.
>
> With that said, she was an outstanding teacher. It was in her class where I really began to learn. We were quizzed and drilled in spelling, reading, writing, and arithmetic, plus learning to multiply and divide.

THIRD GRADE, 1962-1963 (CONTINUED)

MRS. WARJONEN took us on walking field trips to the Timberland Children's Library where we checked out a book for our oral and written book reports. We also participated in the school's spelling B's. We would practice in front of the class, which would determine who would compete. Scholastic Weekly Readers were also read aloud.

During art classes, she emphasized for us to do our best as one of our pictures would be displayed in the yearly Art Gallery Show, held in the gymnasium. Ribbons were awarded and parents were invited to the viewing. Our brother, Doug, won first place for his class artwork that year.

We also experienced history during her class. First were the "duck-and-cover" drills. The United States was in a heated nuclear arms race with the Soviet Union. Our government stressed the need for the public to prepare with extra food and water and even fall-out shelters. In school, drills were performed. A loud warning-bell alerted the children to get under their desks and stay there until the teacher instructed them to crawl out and take their seats. These drills continued for months.

The assassination of President Kennedy brought such sadness to our country that it became a teaching moment as well. Large televisions on tall rolling stands were placed into every classroom—third grade through sixth—and used when we watched the president's funeral in silence. Throughout the year, science and space programs were also viewed on these televisions.

After such solemn times, Mrs. Warjonen must have wanted to provide a more positive experience when we returned from the Christmas holiday. She announced that our class assignment would be to bring an item for "Show and Tell."

FOR CHRISTMAS, Karen and I had both received a Barbie Doll case. Many third-graders didn't know much about Barbie, but I did because of my sister. Soon as she got a Barbie, I got one too. We had such fun playing together, everything centered around the doll.

THIRD GRADE
(SHOW AND TELL)

My sister immediately began designing clothes to put in her case: a red stretch-stocking into an evening gown and a white washcloth into a dress. I was convinced that she'd one day become a famous designer and couldn't have been more pleased when she allowed me to include her creations with my "Show and Tell."

Mrs. Warjonen had placed a long table at the front of the classroom to display our items. My black-vinyl Barbie case became an immediate hit with the girls. As I opened the wardrobe closets inside the case, showing the three accessory drawers filled with Barbie gloves, shoes, and hats, Mrs. Warjonen allowed the girls to come up for a closer look. I then removed my pony-tailed Barbie and her sister, Skipper, from the case and told their history.

At the end of my "Show and Tell," all of the girls clapped. Even Mrs. Warjonen. That day, I made Barbie popular and gained a lot of new friends.

Barbie case and my sister's homemade Barbie outfits.
(Authors' collection)

FOURTH GRADE
Emerson Grade School
Hoquiam, Washington
Story by: Diane Taylor

MRS. SHRAUGER was the same fourth-grade teacher to my brother, Doug, from 1960-1961. To me, her teaching style was exceptional. Not only did she expand the basics, she presented many of the subjects with challenges, providing clues for us to figure out. At times, she'd put us in pairs or teams.

OUR BROTHER, Doug, and his best friend, Danny Kristrom, had been inseparable since kindergarten. To the point where we viewed Danny as a second brother. It was our father who introduced the boys to nature and taught them to hunt, fish, and camp. As positive as this friendship became, it opened up schemes that one might not try on their own. It was in Mrs. Shrauger's class where they devised, what they thought, a full-proof plan. After all it was Spring, too nice to be sitting in class!

Every other day or so, they would appear in the morning class, and after lunch, head to the ponds to watch the ducks and search for polliwogs. When the ending school-bell rang, Danny would cleverly mingle into the line to catch the school bus home while Doug meandered in the opposite direction. This routine lasted a few days before Mrs. Shrauger noticed the pattern. She reported it to Principal Krekow, which sent him on an immediate hunt for the boys.

Principal Krekow found them in the furthermost pond from the school, jumping in the water trying to catch bullfrogs. The boys didn't realize his presence until he grabbed both by their ears. Keeping his grip tight on their earlobes, he pulled and scolded them all the way back to school. The boys were grounded for months and forced to stay after school to complete all their lessons. They also received a hacking from Mr. Krekow's sturdy wooden paddle.

After school, Mrs. Shrauger spent extra time with the two and challenged them with special lessons. Even teamed them up to figure out arithmetic problems.

FOURTH GRADE
Story by: Diane Taylor

When I interviewed my brother about his school memories, he said that if he had to name *one teacher* who truly influenced him to do better, it was Mrs. Shrauger.

After the fourth grade, we noticed a change in Doug. He began to excel in math and history. When Mr. Jones arrived as the athletic director, it was the first time Doug turned out for school sports. In the fifth grade, he became a member of the school-boy patrol. When his sixth-grade teacher, Mrs. Lewis, was trying to form a band, he learned to play the harmonica and received an "A" in music.

DOUG

DANNY
(Authors' collection)

**DOUG'S
EMERSON GRADE SCHOOL
Fourth-grade Report Card
(1960-1961)**
(Authors' collection)

ˣ In 1988, Mrs. Shrauger became Hoquiam's first and only female mayor and served two terms.

CHRISTMAS TREES for school.

Every year, our dad took us Christmas-tree hunting in the woods. It was an adventure finding that perfect tree and one for Grandma and Aunt Eva too. Even the neighbors would put in a request.

The school trees all started when our brother announced that his fifth-grade teacher, Mr. Griffen, had given him permission to bring a tree for his classroom to decorate. Doug was going to use his cub scout training to cut it down.

Diane and I wanted trees for our classrooms and so did the neighborhood kids who had joined us that year in our Christmas-tree hunt. Our dad and brother had to make multiple trips in our old Woody station wagon to retrieve all of the selected trees.

When Principal Krekow got wind of these classroom trees, he put in an order for two large Firs. One for the Gymnasium /Cafeteria and the other for the main lobby. Over the next several years, Principal Krekow was always one of the first with his tree request.

DOUG, Cub Scout
(Authors' collection)

PRINCIPAL KREKOW
Hesperian

EMERSON ELEMENTARY SCHOOL
FOOTBALL, BASKETBALL AND TRACK
ACTIVITIES AWARD CERTIFICATE (1963)
Signed by Larry R. Jones and Principal Krekow

MARBLES BECAME A BIG HIT on the playground of Emerson Grade School. All through the twentieth century, until World War II rationing, it was one of the most popular games for boys.

Marbles date back to as far as the Egyptian tombs, but the origins are unknown. Native American tribes also played a version of the game. Mass production began in Akron, Ohio in 1884 and was perfected in 1915.

Experienced players used the proper nicknames. Aggies or shooters referred to the larger marbles to knock the smaller ones around. The smaller ones had names too: mibs, ducks, and the yellow and black striped ones were called bumblebees.

GLASS-COLORED MARBLES
Emerson Grade School
Story by: Diane Taylor

OUR BROTHER, DOUG, now in fifth-grade, caught on to the game like a pro and moved up the marble ranks as one of the group leaders. Since second grade, Doug's pockets were often loaded with colored marbles that rubbed, creaked, and screeched as he walked.

During recess, marbles covered the ground as boys of all ages practiced the art of shooting. One afternoon, Mr. Griffen, the fifth-grade teacher, appeared at recess. First to observe, then he offered advice, and shortly after, demonstrated the strategy of how to win.

After school, games were organized at the Lamb's Foundry parking lot, which was a quick walk across Emerson Avenue from the school. Lambs was also the location where they would find "steelies." Steelies were marble-size steel balls inside of a bearing which were manufactured at the foundry. Steelies were often used as a prime shooter for the game.

To play a game, teams were formed. The more experienced boys, one being Doug and the others, Watson and Luther, were the team captains. Doug recalled having the Fullerton Brothers, Suther, and Grimsley on his team. They won many championships, and in addition to gaining more marbles, they earned bragging rights at school and around town.

> ### GLASS-COLORED MARBLES (CONTINUED)
> Story by: Diane Taylor
>
> The game was kept simple. With a piece of chalk, they'd draw a large circle on the ground. Each player would have ten marbles of a chosen color and clump them in the middle of the circle. A coin flip or "rock, scissors, paper" would be used to determined which team would start.
>
> Using the fist knuckles-down-to-the-ground method, the player would flick the shooter marble with their thumb, hoping to knock one of the opponent's smaller marbles out of the circle. As long as that player continued knocking marbles out, he'd get another turn. Once he missed, a rivaling team player would play. The winner with the most opposing team's marbles bumped out of the circle, would win. Sometimes, they'd play for keeps where the winning team would keep all of the losing team's marbles, but usually it was left to which team had the highest count. They would also trade marbles, like they did with baseball cards.

AT RECESS, children were encouraged to go outside for fresh air and exercise. One primary and one upper-grade teacher were supposed to be on duty at all times. In bad weather, each room played in designated areas. Recess occurred two times daily for all students: first through sixth grade. The morning session was 10:15 to 10:30 a.m. and the afternoon from 2:00 to 2:15 p.m.

During recess, there were rules for the play equipment. For the monkey bars, upper-grade students could use them in the morning, and the primary classes in the afternoon. Noon was a free time for anyone who ate lunch at school. When on the bars, they had to move in the same direction, plus there was no walking or sitting on the bars. The two tether-ball stations were designated by grades: the one nearest the grandstand was for the primary grades and the one on the east end for the upper grades. The merry-go-round was for the primary students only.

Except for sitting on the grandstand's first and second seats, the grandstand and football field was off limits. Most of these rules were directed to the boys, which included staying off of the grandstand roof and no playing under it, and to stay off of the football field. There was an outfield at the far perimeter where they were allowed to play such games as kickball.

> RECESS
> Emerson Grade School
> Hoquiam, Washington
> Story by: Diane Taylor
>
> STORED IN THE HALL near the door were the jump ropes, basket balls, and balls for kickball. Soon as the recess bell rang, kids jumped from their seats and headed out the door.
>
> In our primary years, first through second grade, the merry-go-round was the favorite attraction unless some mischievous kid got involved. They'd push and hop on with the rest of us, but in mid turn, slide off and start pushing the merry-go-round faster and faster until some of us riders got so dizzy, we'd be forced to slip off and take a hard landing on the ground. We'd then slow the merry-go-round for the others to get off. If this prankster was caught by the recess monitor, he or she would be escorted to the principal's office, but more times than not, the sly kid would make a joke of it and walk off.
>
> As we got older, the boys headed to the outfield for kickball or played marbles or a game of HORSE in basketball. Some of the girls created games with their colored chalk by drawing a hopscotch, tic-tac-toe, or four-square outline on the cement. Double-Dutch jump rope was popular for those skilled enough to master two ropes. When they did, those nearby would either watch or sing along with the ditty:
>
> *Polly put the kettle on, fast as you can.*
> *Faster, faster, fast as you can.*
> *Polly put the kettle on, fast as you can!*

> ### RECESS (CONTINUED)
> Story by: Diane Taylor
>
> RECESS MONITORS for the older kids weren't always within view. Even though we weren't supposed to, we'd sneak underneath the old wooden stadium and go on a treasurer hunt. It was especially fruitful after a sporting event. Coins dropped from a spectator's pockets were the most common found prize and sometimes jewelry or a pack of new gum.
>
> THE FIFTEEN-MINUTE RECESS passed all too quickly. The rush to return to class was not at the same pace of the initial recess bell telling us to go play. Classmates meandered back into the classroom. We had a five-minute grace period to return to our seats. Those who were excessively tardy, were scolded and warned. Then there were some who required fetching, which usually followed with a visit to the principal's office.

ON THE LAST DAY of school in June, every student from Emerson Grade School was treated to a year-end picnic at Lions Park. Each class followed their teacher, single-file, as they walked along the side street of Adams and up the Chenault hill to the park. The classes connected to the other with a teacher in between and became so long that we looked like a trail of ants.

As we approached the park, we were greeted by the large wooden sign that read LIONS PARK and was leaning against the front rock embankment. With a backdrop of cedar, hazelnut, and hemlock trees, plus its meadow of buttercups and daisies, the park had become nature's playground for children, family picnics, and community events for many years.

PICTURESQUE ON A HILLSIDE, Lions Park was located at the top of west Chenault Avenue and Endresen Road and overlooked Grays Harbor Bay. It was built by the Hoquiam's Lions Club, which was officially charted by the Lions Club International in February 1942. The international organization was initially formed in 1917 by Chicago business leader, Melvin Jones, whose idea of people putting their talents together to improve their communities took hold. As his message spread, a motto was adopted: "Where there's a need, there's a Lion."

ONCE HOQUIAM'S Lions club secured a site, the making of one of the most spectacular community parks was started in the early 1950s. For the children, a fifteen-foot swing-set, equipped with eight swings, was erected. The chain-linked swings connected to U-shaped seats and became one of the highlights for children and adults alike. With such long chains, participants could pump their legs to such heights that their toes almost touched the top limbs of the alders.

LIONS PARK SWING SET
(Authors' collection)

Other play apparatus included: a metal slide with a long journey down, an over-sized merry-go-round that could hold ten or more, monkey bars large enough for five to six kids to swing across from bar to bar or hang from their knees. The two long teeter-totters were of equal fun, but required a trusted partner, not one who liked to slide off at the bottom, shooting the up-in-the-air person down with a loud thump and stinging rump.

The baseball field and sand-filled horseshoe pits offered a place for challenging games. The picnic tables, scattered near the covered pavilion, which housed a brick cook-stove grill, provided plenty of seating. Six or so picnic tables were also inside the pavilion for those picnicking on a rainy day. Two waist-high water fountains built into square rock-slab bases provided a side step for a thirsty child to reach for a drink. A block lavatory building stood at the edge of the park, one side for "boys" and the other "girls," and hid trails behind it that were enjoyed by the boys for exploring. Yearly, Emerson and Lincoln Grade schools used the park for their year-end picnics.

LIONS PARK PICNIC
Emerson Grade School Early 1960s
Hoquiam, Washington
Story by: Diane Taylor

UPON ARRIVAL TO LIONS PARK, the children scattered but were always under the watchful eye of the principal, volunteer mothers, and teachers using megaphones, whistles, and binoculars. Whistles, signified "stop," and many times were followed with voices through the megaphones, hollering commands.

IN THE OPEN MEADOW, gunny-sack relay races, plus baseball and kickball games were formed. Others headed to the swings, merry-go-round, and monkey bars. Some of the boys, including our brother, snuck off to the hillside trail behind the lavatory.

The top of the trail butted up to a steep embankment with large tree roots protruding from the dirt and vines hanging from the top. One by one, each boy with a running start up the hill, would grab hold of the tree root or a vine, and if able, shinny himself to the top of the ridge. Once he reached it, he'd holler "Billy-goat, gruff," before skidding back down and repeating the "gruff" mantra as dirt and mud landed on his clothes and in his hair. Then back in line for another turn.

WHEN THE LOUD CLANG of the cast-iron triangle dinner-bell ricocheted across the park, herds of running feet from every direction raced to their designated class line. Hot dogs and hamburgers with pork and beans and potato chips were served by the cook staff and volunteers. Later, the dessert treat was an Eskimo Pie ice-cream bar.

By three o'clock, we headed back to school for a final headcount and then were dismissed for the summer break.

CHAPTER 13
LINCOLN ELEMENTARY SCHOOL

IN 1907, FORTY-SIX voters turned out to pass an initiative for a two-story, four-room schoolhouse in the northern section of town. Same as McKinley, the land for the Lincoln School was procured from Hoquiam pioneer, James A. Karr. Shortly after the purchase, all the key players aligned: Aberdeen architect, C.E. Troutman, drew the plans; Sneider and Lindahl cleared the land; the Grays Harbor Construction company laid the bricks, and Grays Harbor Railway and Light, with their $260,000 accepted bid, wired the building.

The new school, which provided six classrooms for about 150 students, was seated high on a mound with tranquil views of lumber ships sailing past along the Hoquiam River. It also became a prideful community foundation for the hard-working people living in the northern outskirts of town.

LINCOLN ELEMENTARY
(Courtesy of the Polson Museum, Hoquiam, Wash., 2005.030.0049)

LINCOLN ELEMENTARY STUDENTS (1910)
(Courtesy of the Polson Museum, Hoquiam, Wash., 2010.036.0172)

IN SEPTEMBER 1908, Principal Albert Gibbons and his staff: Miss Rundell, Miss June Copeland, and Miss Emma Mark, welcomed Lincoln School's first students. Included were children from the Grays Harbor City school, which had been absorbed into the Hoquiam School District. The new school offered opportunity to those who would have never made the long trek to attend McKinley. In celebration of the new school, the Women's Relief Corporation had sewn the American flag, which was now flying high above on the front pole.

LINCOLN ELEMENTARY BASEBALL TEAM (1910)
BASEBALL TEAM
(Courtesy of the Polson Museum, Hoquiam, Wash., 1977.028.0006)

By 1915, a large student growth necessitated the addition of a top story with four additional classrooms, which now accommodated 100 more students. The new student headcount was 250. (*The Age of Enrollment and Space*, Lincoln School, *Courtesy of Larry R. Jones' collection*).

LINCOLN ELEMENTARY SCHOOL
WITH THE THIRD STORY
(Courtesy of the Polson Museum, Hoquiam, Wash., 2001.018.0127)

With another growth, a back addition was added in 1929, which added two more classrooms, an auditorium, a library, and two storage rooms. The student headcount had increased to 300. With approximately eight teachers in the 1930's, one being the principal teaching sixth grade, each teacher handled approximately thirty-seven pupils. One must assume that these additional classrooms provided a study hall for some of the overflow students.

One month after school had started in September 1929, the stock market crashed, October 29th, and had spiraled the nation into a serious depression that lasted a decade. All communities were impacted, including the schools. Budgets were tightened, which added extra workload for the teachers and staff.

By 1934, all four Taylor kids: Rose, Carmelita, Virginia, and our father, young Paul, were attending Lincoln Elementary. They lived on Endresen Road along the Hoquiam River. That same year, Grandpa Cline built an eighteen-foot skiff equipped with a sail that reshaped the family's life. The kids named the boat *Skookum* and used it to row themselves to Lincoln School.

On May 23, 1934, Mother (Agnes) and the children treated guests to a picnic. They picked them up in their rowboat at the dock nearest to the school. The children invited several of their teachers and young Paul included two of his friends.

Excerpt from Agnes Taylor's (née Cline) boat Log: [1]

> **LOG OF THE SKOOKUM, MAY 23, 1934**
> **18' Skiff and Sail**
> **Built by Fred Cline, Humptulips, Washington**
> Log entries by Agnes Taylor (née Cline)
>
> *I took the boat down to Karr Avenue dock, got there at 3:20 p.m. Hard pull the last half hour against Nor'wester. At 6:30, the children and I took cake and sandwiches and had as guests:* **Mrs. Edmondson and Miss Turman, first and second-grade teachers,** *plus Ora Turner, Virginia Winters, Joe Winters, and Bob Edmonson. We rowed up river to Robert Gray Mill and got out on green grass and built a fire, made tea, and ate lunch. Later rowed to dock by American Door Mill dock. The teachers got out with the boys and the rest of us went on up to our landing.*

LINCOLN ELEMENTARY FIRST GRADE 1934
TEACHER: MRS. EDMONDSON
First-grade student, Paul Taylor, (Authors' father)
(Authors' collection)

TAYLOR KIDS (Sept 1934)
First day of school at Lincoln Elementary
L to R: Rose, Carmelita, Virginia, and Paul
(Authors' collection)

PAUL TAYLOR
Second-grade drawing
(Authors' collection)

BY 1938, PRINCIPAL POYHONEN[y] had carried Lincoln through the Depression for almost eight years. One can be assured that budgets and schedules continued to be tight. In his report to the Board of Education, he outlined the wearing of multiple hats, as well as teaching sixth grade. Excerpt from his report:

> *Under the present set-up, the principal's position is somewhat that of a building "head-teacher." The principal carries a full classroom*

---

[y] By the mid 1940's, Principal Poyhonen was working as an attorney in his own practice in Hoquiam. In 1950, he was appointed to the position of Grays Harbor County Superior Court Judge.

teaching load, and his non-classroom activities must necessarily be limited to general building control assignment of special duties, taking care of difficult cases of discipline, conferences with building teachers.

His general comment about the Lincoln Elementary teachers provided positive views. He stated that they had all worked in harmony with his staff and showed a willingness and professional manner to help with additional tasks. These included P.T.A activities, playfield and lunchroom supervision, and prompt reporting of their work. He viewed their age, all under thirty-five, as a benefit. "Loss of efficiency due to old age is not involved," he wrote.

TEACHER	GRADE	ASSESSMENT
Miss Helen Holcomb	First grade	a. In second year of service.
		b. Inclined to be officious/bossy.
		c. Sincere, hard worker.
		d. Satisfactory relations with parents, pupils, and staff.
		e. Holds four-year degree in Primary education.

TEACHER	GRADE	ASSESSMENT
Miss Ruth Moller	First grade	a. One and one-half years.
		b. Youngest teacher, 22-23 yrs.
		c. Conscientious.
		d. A little above average teacher.
		e. Holds two-year certificate.
		f. Continuing education, summer courses, Bellingham, to earn her teaching diploma.

TEACHER	GRADE	ASSESSMENT
Miss Helen Turman	Second grade	a. Seven years of service. b. Previous three-year disability resolved, improved health. c. Worked harder these past two years. d. More "easy-going" than the other teachers. e. Holds two-year certificate. f. Completed six-week summer course, San Francisco State Teacher's College, 1936.

TEACHER	GRADE	ASSESSMENT
Miss Martha Jensen	Split second and third grade	a. First year of service. b. Hard worker. c. Maintains good discipline. d. Cheerfully accepts assignments. e. Works well with others. f. Completed six-week summer course, 1937, University of Washington.

TEACHER	GRADE	ASSESSMENT
Miss Mary Fosjack	Third grade	a. Seven years of service. b. Punctual in her work. c. Maintains good order. d. Cheerfully accepts assignments. e. Professional training since becoming a teacher at Lincoln. f. Completed twelve-week summer course, 1930, Bellingham Normal. In the winter of 1935, was granted a leave of absence to attend the University of Washington.

TEACHER	GRADE	ASSESSMENT
Miss Emily Henningsen	Fourth grade	a. Seven years of service.
		b. Conscientious.
		c. Maintains good order.
		d. Competent.
		e. Consistently makes adequate preparation in her teaching.
		f. Attended one summer course.
		g. In 1935, took a quarter's work at the University of Portland.

TEACHER	GRADE	ASSESSMENT
Miss Judith Ring	Fifth grade	a. Second year of service.
		b. Slightly old-maidish, but not crabby.
		c. Considerable work in dramatics and auditorium programs. Taken lead role in these activities.
		d. Well-liked, courteous, pleasant.
		e. Good worker
		f. Attended twelve-week summer course, University of Washington 1936.

IN 1956, LINCOLN ELEMENTARY received its renovation go-ahead after the passing of the $600,000 bond presented to voters on March 8, 1955. The first to be completed was the building of a multi-purpose room, adding an auditorium and physical education facility. Next came the renovations and restructures. These included the creation of a kindergarten from a previous store-room and a classroom moved into the auditorium and into the library. The remedial class relocated into a small office. The office went into a store room, and two small rooms were created, one for a nurse's room and the other for the women teachers.

Prior to the completion of the gym, the basketball team practiced in the hallways. Their school colors were red and black and their mascot, the Abe's. Named after Abraham Lincoln.

The old cafeteria had been moved into a larger classroom. The previous cafeteria had been moved in 1943 to a 30'x30' former classroom and outgrew its space. By 1951, the school was feeding an average of 160 students. By 1964, the cafeteria student-count had increased to 187. Classrooms and the hallway accommodated for the cold-lunch eaters. A 1957 Lincoln student stated that the cafeteria cooks made some of the best food he ever ate. It was all homemade, including the fresh baked bread and cinnamon rolls.

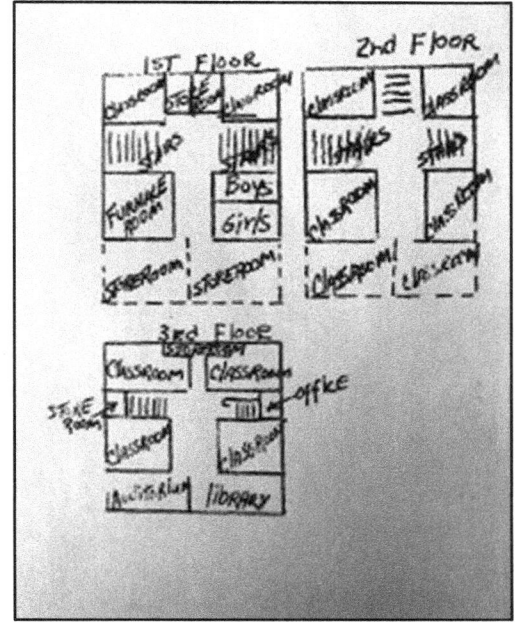

LINCOLN ELEMENTARY 1955 RECONFIGURATION
The Age of Enrollment and Space
(Courtesy of Larry R. Jones' collection)

With these renovations, problems arose: the small lunch room was too close to the lavatory, the two lavatories—one for boys and one for girls—weren't adequate, and the small women's room only had one small lavatory and the men teachers had none. Store room space had been eaten up, the playground had grown smaller, and three drinking fountains were not sufficient. The remedial room, which had been forced into a smaller room, was now sandwiched between two classrooms and picked up every sound. [2]

AFTER GRADUATING COLLEGE IN 1957, Harborite, Larry Jones, returned to Grays Harbor to teach sixth grade at Lincoln Elementary.

Larry taught at Lincoln for three years, then enrolled at the University of Oregon in Eugene for postgraduate studies. In the fall of 1960, he was hired by Emerson Elementary School as both the sixth-grade teacher of math, history, and science as well as the athletic director.

151

**LINCOLN ELEMENTARY
(1957-1960)
Sixth-grade class with
Teacher, Larry Jones**
(Courtesy of Larry R. Jones' collection)

LINCOLN SCHOOL SKIT (1959)

Back Row (LtoR): Art Irion (parent), **Larry Jones (teacher)**,
Vic Fletcher (parent), **Walt Chapman (Principal)**
Front Row (LtoR): Lane Fletcher (brother of Vic),
Ray (Junior) Dalrymple (parent)
(Courtesy of Larry R. Jones' collection)

AFTER THE UNEXPECTED passing of Lincoln Elementary Principal, Walter Chapman, in 1963, Larry Jones was approached by his mentor, Principal Krekow of Emerson Elementary to apply for the position. "You're ready," Mr. Krekow had told him. Before Larry knew it, he was setting up office in the 1907 basement of the old Lincoln School. He was Lincoln's principal for a total of fourteen years, September 1963 through June 1977. Five of those years at the old school and nine at the new one. For years to come, he was the youngest principal in the Hoquiam school district to hold that position.

AS PRINCIPAL, MR. JONES performed all administrative tasks. There was no secretary. In addition to his principal duties of handling the school, he answered all incoming phone calls, handled all money transactions, including school lunches, delivered messages, and administered discipline to unruly children when needed. With the help of the teachers, he also organized field trips and school events, such as the annual school carnival, the Halloween party, and one of his favorites, the year-end Christmas production.

LINCOLN SCHOOL ARTIFACT
(Courtesy of Larry R. Jones' collection)

ONE YEAR, to celebrate the history of Thanksgiving, the Lincoln students dressed as Pilgrims for a field trip to Taholah. When their bus reached their destination, the Pilgrims were greeted by the Native-American children in garments honoring their cultural heritage. Pupils from each group reenacted the Thanksgiving feast.

THE ABERDEEN and Hoquiam school districts developed a cross-cultural workshop. The purpose was to better acquaint the teachers and parents with the history, culture and current concerns and perspectives of the local Native-Americans. Particular emphasis was placed on the Native-American child in the local schools. Lincoln Principal Larry Jones is pictured in the school-district newsletter, *Keeping Tabs*, at a workshop with the Taholah and Quinault Education Committee members.

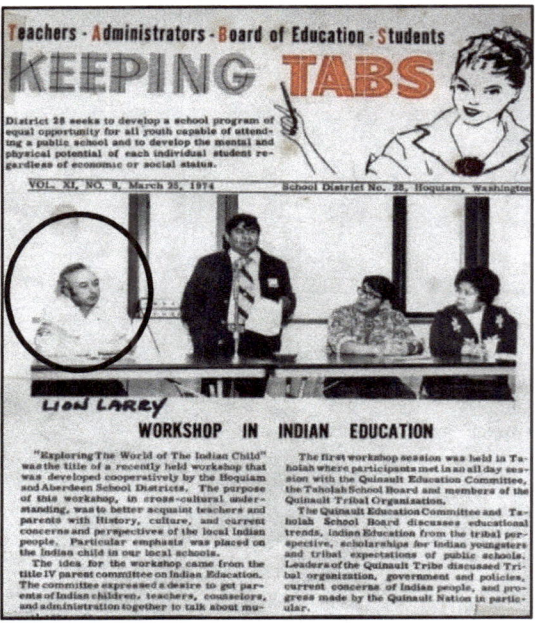

**LARRY JONES WITH TAHOLAH AND QUINAULT
COMMITTEE MEMBERS AT WORKSHOP**
(Courtesy of Larry R. Jones' collection)

Pictured (below) is the committee of school officials and members of the Native-American community who signed an application for a federal grant to fund a joint project through school year 1973-74 under the heading of "Contemporary Problems in the Native-American Education."

Front Row (LtoR): Dan Jackson, of Chippewa heritage and student at Hoquiam High School; Mrs. Shirley Ralston, Co-chairman, parent and of Quinault heritage; Mrs. Irene Black, Co-chairman, parent, and of Chehalis heritage, John Nold, Asst. Admin. of Pupil Services for Aberdeen schools.
Back Row (LtoR): Larry Jones, Lincoln School Principal in Hoquiam and Mrs. Marlene Dixon of Aberdeen, Title I Liaison, parent, and of Quinault heritage.
(Courtesy of Larry R. Jones' collection)

DURING THE CHRISTMAS holiday, a large tree, which was usually furnished by one of the students' relatives, was placed on the main floor, often a Silver Fir at least fifteen-feet high. It required the assistance of the maintenance crew to bedeck. On the morning before the Christmas break, the children gathered around this ornamented giant tree and sat before it by class level: kindergarteners first, then first grade, second grade, and so on. Teacher Dorothye Logue, at the piano, began her recital of well-known Christmas tunes. With the children singing and her piano keys rattling "Jingle Bells and Rudoph the Red-nose Reindeer," plus other tunes, an acoustical magic reverberated through the halls and up to the ceiling.

LINCOLN SCHOOL held its year-end picnic at Lion's Park. It was a long walk. Each class followed their teacher south on Lincoln Avenue, up and over Sunset Hill, to and along Chenault Avenue, and then up another hill to the park.

Pictured at Lions Park are Lincoln Principal Larry Jones and Sixth-grade teacher, Ed Rosi. Ed Rosi later became Lincoln's principal.

LIONS PARK (1964)
Principal Larry Jones and
Ed Rosi (Sixth-grade Teacher)
(Courtesy of Larry R. Jones' collection)

Lions Park caretaker's home in background.

AT THE END of the 1950s decade, the Hoquiam School Board's 1951 school-renovation plan had completed two of its three phases. In 1962, the third phase was resurrected, which encompassed the replacement of two public schools: Lincoln Elementary and Hoquiam High School. Once a budget was developed and two bonds and special levies passed, the project moved forward.

On June 7, 1968, the old Lincoln School said goodbye to its last students. In August that same year, the new single-level Lincoln School, around the bend, welcomed its new pupils. A dedication and open house were held on October 1, 1968, with welcoming ceremonies presented by Principal Larry Jones.

LINCOLN ELEMENTARY STAFF, 1970-1971
(Courtesy of the Polson Museum, Hoquiam, Wash.2015.086.0002)
Front row: (LtoR): 4th from left (polka dot dress) **Dorothye Logue**;
5th from left, **Principal Larry Jones**
Second Row: (LtoR): 1st from left (pink sweater) **Eileen Kosoff** (Asst. Cook)

LINCOLN ELEMENTARY STAFF, 1970-1971
BACK OF PHOTO
(Courtesy of the Polson Museum, Hoquiam, Wash.2015.086.0002-2)

OLD LINCOLN SCHOOL DEMOLITION
MID 1970s
(Courtesy of the Polson Museum, Hoquiam, Wash. 2018.096.0001)

This photo was taken by the Kosoff family. Eileen Kosoff was an assistant cook at Lincoln for almost twenty years. Her husband Monte and his siblings plus their children attended Lincoln Elementary. Their son, Tracy, went on to be a highly-decorated Naval Submarine Captain.

CHAPTER 14
WASHINGTON SCHOOL

WASHINGTON SCHOOL (1908)
(Courtesy of the Polson Museum, Hoquiam, Wash., 2005.030.0029)

WASHINGTON SCHOOL opened its doors in 1908. Unlike McKinley and Lincoln, which taught only through the sixth grade, Washington School extended classes through the eighth grade. For some students, eighth grade would be the highest formal education they would pursue.

Those attending high school had a long walk to Central No. 1, which required crossing the river at the Eighth Street Bridge or transport by boat or ferry.

**WASHINGTON SCHOOL, 1908-1909
ELLA D. NICHOL'S SECOND AND THIRD GRADE CLASSES**
(Courtesy of the Polson Museum, Hoquiam, Wash.,2001.018.0131)

**WASHINGTON SCHOOL 1913 BASKETBALL CHAMPS
WITH PRINCIPAL DUTTON**
Bloomquist, Hubble, Sandgren, Dolk, Winkle (Capt.)
(Courtesy of the Polson Museum, Hoquiam, Wash., 2007.003.0617)

**WASHINGTON SCHOOL, 1914
THIRD-GRADE CLASS**
(Courtesy of the Polson Museum, Hoquiam, Wash., 2016.081.0006)

DUE TO WASHINGTON SCHOOL's offsite location, it was organized like a rural school, teaching through the eighth grade. The other Hoquiam elementary schools stopped at sixth. They continued this format until 1935.

MISS DRURY'S SEVENTH-GRADE CLASS (Circa 1920)
(Courtesy of the Polson Museum, Hoquiam, Wash., 2006.058.0134)

IN 1935, WASHINGTON SCHOOL had a major restructure. They would no longer be teaching seventh and eighth grades. For the first time this age group would be making the long walk over the bridge to Hoquiam Junior High. This same year, Principal Franklin retired and was replaced with Principal Reese.[1] This change occurred during the Depression years, but it is unknown if this restructure was a result of budget cuts or of changing teaching methods.

WASHINGTON FOLLOWED the same format as the other elementary schools: one teacher for each grade-level. With no public-school kindergarten yet, five and six-year-olds were enrolled into the first grade. The *Dick and Jane* books were among the lessons taught. Most of the teachers were women. In 1935, they had one man teacher, Mr. Howard, who taught sixth grade.

When second-grade teacher, Miss Swanson, left in 1936 to marry, she was forced to quit her job. The Washington State law, mandating that married women could not teach, was later changed in the 1940s during WWII, due to a teacher shortage.[2]

EVERY CLASSROOM AT Washington had a cloak room with assigned hooks for each student. The children would bring jump ropes, roller skates, and balls to school. These items had to be hung or placed under the assigned hooks. The roller skates were used only as transport to and from school, but never in the hallways or used at recess. For the younger children, grades one through four, they could place their balls in their inkwells. The older children, grades five and six, now using the inkwells, stored their balls inside their desks. Depending on the teacher, if a ball got loose in class, it was never seen again.[3]

During recess, the children played outside. On rainy days, they headed to the large play shed. It had a solid floor and a roof and kept the children dry, but also became so crowded that no one could hardly move. The children also had play seasons that never intertwined. The girls had jump-rope season, hop-scotch season, and ball season at the end of the year. The boys shot marbles, and played basketball and softball. If it was really stormy, the students would stay in their current classroom and amuse themselves with games.[4]

BY THE EARLY 1940s, Washington had a public-school kindergarten, which Mary Lillegard (née Williams) attended in 1945. Same as her older sister, three years prior, and her younger brother, two years after.

Mary recalled Washington School's magnificent wooden staircase leading up to the third floor and the spacious classrooms with wood-framed windows and private cloak rooms. Their playground had a baseball field, swings, and the large covered open-air play shed, where a small team of girls played wall-ball and hop scotch, plus other games. Games were no longer played by season.

Mary's fifth-grade teacher, Mr. Shrauger, was considered one of the best, and Principal Bargewell sported a mustache and graying hair. She remembered that Washington had a good basketball team and that she was always seated at the back of the classroom because her name began with a "W." Her mother was an active member of the school's PTA. In fact, she never missed a meeting, but had to bring the kids with her, so she hid them in the school kitchen. "Play quiet," she would say.

MARY AND HER SIBLINGS plus single mother, lived with their grandmother on the 29th block of Pacific Avenue in Hoquiam. There were no nearby houses, only open fields from Pacific Avenue toward the railroad tracks and beyond to the bay. Their closest neighbor had cows and chickens.

Periodically, the neighbor would give Mary's family a jar of cream that she and her siblings shook until it turned into butter. Every Thanksgiving Day, they could hear the commotion of the annual Aberdeen vs Hoquiam game from their grandmother's porch.

When the carnival or circus came to town, it would set up in the open grassy fields, just a block or so from Mary's grandmother's house. Once the carnival ended and was breaking down its tents and structures, some of the workers permitted several of the young boys, one being Mary's brother, to wait nearby. As the trucks pulled out, the boys were waved on to scour through the sawdust, sifting through it for dropped coins.

CARVINAL IN OPEN FIELDS OFF PACIFIC AVE, HOQUIAM
(Courtesy of the Polson Museum, Hoquiam, Wash. 2009.003.0938)

During WWII, Mary's mother delivered the mail, but once the war ended, she lost her job. In between permanent jobs, money was tight, but Mary's mother always found work. She later hired on at the chair factory.

When Mary and her siblings needed new shoes for school, mother and the kids headed to the hills behind the PUD building and picked wild blackberries. The Morck Hotel, paying $3.00 a gallon, earned the family twenty-four dollars.

Almost every morning, Mary's mother escorted the children to school. When they entered Hoquiam Junior High, she walked them to the Simpson Avenue Bridge.

There were no school buses transporting students across the river to the high school compound. Some parents drove their children there, others paid 5 cents to ride the intercity bus, but most of the kids walked. For Mary and her siblings, it was over a four-mile round trip from home to school and back.

The Washington School students, who lived along Simpson Avenue or south of it, used the large Simpson Avenue Bridge to the Hoquiam High School compound. Those closer to Sumner Avenue and toward the hill took the alternate route along Riverside to the shorter Eighth Street Bridge.

The Eighth Street Bridge was a swing out and much older than the Simpson Avenue one. Occasionally, people got stuck on the part that swung out and had to be rescued by boat.[5]

The Simpson Avenue Bridge was a draw bridge. Everyone knew that security measures were in place to prevent people from being stuck on the bridge when it opened, but it still caused anxiety to some. It was especially concerning when you crossed onto the section that opened high to the sky when a ship or tall boat approached. Many of the kids increased their pace crossing that segment.

Mary recalled that Laddy, their brown and white wire-haired terrier, was always at the base of the bridge waiting to walk them home. She doesn't know how he knew to be there at that precise time, but regardless of the weather, he was always there to greet them.

Mary attended Hoquiam Junior High from seventh to ninth grade. Her favorite class was PE and Home Economics where she learned to sew. After graduating from the ninth grade in 1955, Mary's family moved to a rustic cabin in Ocosta where she and her brother completed high school. Mary's sister, had graduated from Hoquiam High School in 1955 and relocated to Forks with a neighbor to babysit their children.

ANOTHER STUDENT who attended Washington School in the late 1940s through the early 1950s, under Principal Bargewell's administration, recalled the following:

- Students, who were deemed malnourished or too scrawny, had to report to the nurse's office every morning before class for a spoonful of Cod Liver Oil.

- Once a week, fire drills were conducted to ensure that the school was meeting the standard record time. However, their drills were not like other schools. Washington School had a fire-escape slide, sometimes called chutes, attached to the side of the building at the third floor. It was fully enclosed and looked like a giant rubber hose. When the fire bell shrieked, the entire school: the students, principal, staff, and all of the teachers headed to the third floor and lined up. One by one, they slid down the chute to safety. The student stated: "It was so much fun we couldn't hardly wait until the next week for that bell to ring."

The Washington School fire-escape slide would have been similar to the Aberdeen General Hospital's tubular escape slide, pictured.

Note: In the early 1950s, Washington School still had its old wiring, so extra safety measures, such as this slide, were implemented.

1940 ABERDEEN GENERAL HOSPITAL
Courtesy of the Polson Museum, Hoquiam, Wash., 2021.023.0027)

IN 1956, WASHINGTON SCHOOL received its consent for renovations with the passing of the $600,000 school bond. This included a complete rewiring of the school. The previous 1,000 wattage per classroom was updated to a 3,000 wattage. The play shed was enclosed and converted into a multi-purpose room for free play and physical education. Heat was also added, plus a stage, shower, and dressing rooms. This new auditorium would be open for the public and youth meetings too, such as the Girls Scouts, Boy Scouts, and other community events and organizations.

WASHINGTON SCHOOL FOLLOWED the same activity schedule as the other elementary schools: a yearly carnival, Halloween Parade, and year-end picnic, which in later years was held at the Olympic Stadium. They had sports teams with school colors of blue and gold and named, the Bulldogs. Through the 1950s, most of the kids still crossed the bridges on foot to high school.

SIMPSON AVENUE BRIDGE
DRAW BRIDGE
(Courtesy of the Polson Museum, Hoquiam, Wash.,
1981.046.9001, 2021.023.0234 and 2010.036.0162)

EIGHTH STREET BRIDGE
SWING BRIDGE
(Courtesy of the Polson Museum, Hoquiam, Wash.,
1979.020.0005)

1972 WASHINGTON SCHOOL FIRE
(Courtesy of the Polson Museum, Hoquiam, Wash., 2013.042.0009)

PRIOR TO THE SUMMER break of 1972, a fire erupted in the old Washington School. Every principal was out of town except for Larry Jones, Principal of Lincoln Elementary. When he was alerted about the fire, he rushed over. Upon arrival, he saw people entering the building and hauling out school books. He corralled several to assist him, then led the group downstairs to the principal's office to retrieve school-district records. Back and forth, at least fifteen times, he and the others sloshed through ankle-high water. On his last trip, he spotted a horseshoe hanging upside-down over the principal's door. He pulled it off the wall and set it atop his pile. During this fire rescue, Mr. Jones was still wearing his suit, tie, and good wing-tipped dress shoes.

THE OLD Washington School couldn't be saved and was later demolished. The Hoquiam Junior High School was sectioned off for the displaced Washington School students.

The new Washington School was built in a new location on Cherry Street and opened its doors in 1975.

1975 WASHINGTON SCHOOL
(Courtesy of the Polson Museum, Hoquiam, Wash. 2015.003.0001)

CHAPTER 15
ELEMENTARY SCHOOL COMMONALITIES

DURING THE DEPRESSION of the 1930's, the idea of an indoor school carnival was sparked. Not only as a community booster but a means for the schools to raise funds for school events, sports equipment and uniforms, even specialized study guides or supplies. All of Hoquiam's elementary schools: Central, Emerson, Lincoln, and Washington School planned a carnival as a yearly event.

Merchants and local clubs championed the cause by donating prizes for the games. Billboards were posted on the school walls and in businesses' windows. Leading up to the event, local newspapers advertised the carnival with cartoonlike pictures and credited all of the sponsors.

PTA COMMITTEE members selected a carnival chairman and volunteers, which consisted of both parents and teachers. Parents also headed the publicity and publication of magazines and calendars, all used to advertise the event. Tickets were either bought beforehand or sold at the door.

WEEKS BEFORE the carnival, volunteers congregated at the school, some came to construct the booths and concession stands, while others organized the rooms and finalized the arrangements. The day of and hours before, last-minute set-up was also done.

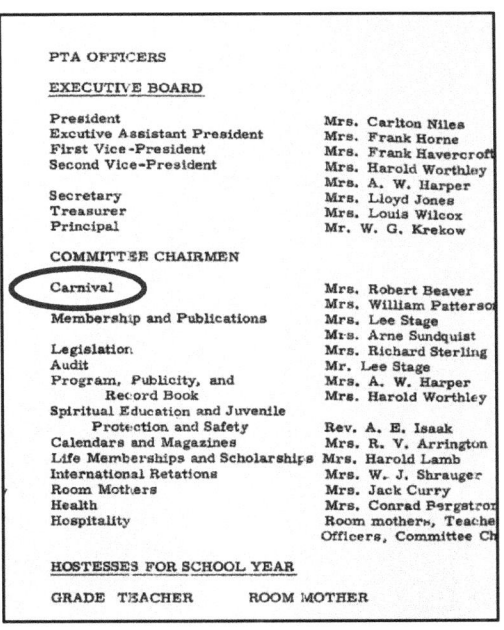

**EMERSON ELEMENTARY
PTA SCHEDULE**
Carnival, February 1961
(Courtesy of Larry R. Jones' collection)

THE EMERSON SCHOOL CARNIVAL in the 1960's was usually held in February on a Thursday or Friday and started at six p.m. Soon as you walked through the school doors, you were transformed into a circus-like festival.

Paper hats, pinwheels, and kazoos were handed out to the children at each entrance as upbeat tunes like the "Baby Elephant Walk" and "The Purple-people Eater," echoed through the airwaves. Red, white, and blue balloons, some purple and yellow ones too, festooned the walls and booths as whiffs of popcorn, cotton candy, and hot dogs, intermingled with heavenly smells. Tables and chairs were scattered throughout for people to sit or to eat a snack purchased from the concession stands, which included ice-cream bars, hot coffee, and soda too. People of all ages, from all areas of town, milled around, in and out of the classrooms, down the halls, and into the gymnasium, trying their wit and skills at these various attractions:

- ❖ The Fish Pond was very popular, especially with the younger kids. Inside the classroom was a tall booth that was decorated with blue-paper waves and crayon-drawn fish, sketched by the primary-grade classes. A volunteer would hand each child a fishing-pole stick, which had a long string with a clothes pin tied to the end. Two or three children could fish at once. Holding their fishing stick, they'd fling the string over the booth wall where a hidden volunteer attached a small toy or candy with the clothes pin. The volunteer then tugged the string up and down, which signaled the child to pull up their stick and claim their prize.

- ❖ The Toilet-paper Toss. Players were given two minutes to continually toss toilet-paper rolls into a cardboard booth shaped like a toilet bowl. The prizes were categorized by successful tosses within the time limit. One to five tosses would earn a prize from shelf one; six to ten tosses from shelf two, and so on. The grand prize of a stuffed animal or doll sat on the very top shelf and were won by few.

- ❖ The Shooting Gallery. Participants shot an air gun at a target nailed to the booth. This event was enjoyed by all and located in the gymnasium. Every successful hit to the target determined which shelf they could pick their prize.

- Dodge-'em baseball required a willing attendant to wear an umpire mask while participants threw a ball at their face. It is assumed that this was played in the early years, but discontinued for fear or result of the booth attendant getting hurt.

- The Roulette Wheel always drew a large crowd and required no skill, just a purchase of a separate ticket and a "lady-luck spin." After cards were handed out, the attendant put the wheel into rotation. The hawk-eyed crowd, now fixated on the wheel whirling round and round, would anxiously wait for the wheel to stop, hopefully on their number. When a lucky participant held up his or her card and was declared the winner, some of the crowd would dissipate, others would buy another ticket for the next spin. The happy winner would head to the table to pick a prize.

- The cake walk became one of the standards throughout the years and followed a similar format of the roulette-wheel game, requiring a separate ticket before each walk. Out-of-order numbered squares were taped to the floor, forming a large circle. As the music started, using bubbly songs like: "Lollipop-Lollipop, Oh, Lolli, Lollipop," the participants would walk from numbered-square to numbered-square until the music suddenly stopped. The cake-walk attendant would then draw a number from a tin canister and call it out. That lucky winner got to choose any cake from a scrumptious assortment of all sizes, shapes, and flavors. Each cake included the baker's name and recipe. The expert bakers were well-known in the community and many carnival-goers flocked to make this their first event. Any left-over goodies were auctioned off at the end of the carnival.

- Guess Your Weight and the Ten-Pin Bowling game was played for a candy surprise.

- The "Dunk Tank," set up in the gymnasium on a large tarp, was built by a local handyman who donated his time and the apparatus for community events. It became one of the most popular attractions, especially if it featured a favorite teacher, like Mr. Jones, who had volunteered several times to be dunked. It was usually the older boys and adults purchasing the separate tickets, then lining up to throw the ball at the bull's-eye. Not sure if there was a direct prize associated, except for the thrill of causing another dunking of the "good sport," who was sitting, quivering-wet, on the diving-board-like platform. When a sharp-shooter ball headed him to the water, followed by a big splash of waves overflowing the glass tank, the crowd erupted with hoots and hollers.

THE SCHOOL-BOY PATROL was an organization of fifth-grade boys commissioned by the State Patrol. They worked directly under the supervision of the City Police Department and the school principal. They were authorized to take charge of private and public vehicle traffic. When they were on duty, the children were to follow their command when crossing the streets.

Every elementary school had formed a patrol and furnished them with belts, flags, and safety-patrol badges while on duty.

WHEN THE AUTOMOBILE first started populating streets, people crossing roads became a precarious situation. The first school to implement a safety program was recorded in St. Paul, Minnesota in 1921. One year prior, AAA president, Charles Hayes, had witnessed a fatal accident involving children, which pushed him to develop a safety program and guidelines for dealing with traffic. The National Congress of Parents and Teachers joined with input, and by the 1930s, the National Safety Council entered the cause. AAA raised greater awareness for the safety patrols by holding rallies and an annual parade in Washington D.C. The organization also originated a pledge:

**EMERSON GRADE SCHOOL
PARENT-TEACHER ASSOCIATION
1961-1962 Rules, Regulations,
and Guidelines**
(Courtesy of Larry R. Jones' collection)

"I pledge to report for duty on time, perform my duties faithfully, strive to prevent accidents, always setting a good example myself, obey my teachers and officers of the patrol, report dangerous student practices, strive to earn the respect of followers."

The official uniform adopted became known as the "Sam Browne belt"— a diagonal strap over the shoulder connected to a seat-belt-like belt buckled at the waist. The name was derived from British general, Sam Browne, who had lost his arm in combat. To steady his sword sheath, he added a shoulder strap.

It was first determined that boys made the best patrol officers, prohibiting girls. By the 1940s, recruitment was opened to everyone.

THE SCHOOL PATROL, 1965
EMERSON GRADE SCHOOL
Story by: Diane Taylor

ONE SPRING DAY in 1965, Police Sergeant Bill attended my fifth-grade class to present safety protocols in crossing streets. He brought training materials, safety flags, and two Sam-Browne belts. After explaining the guidelines and importance of the school patrol, he ushered us outside for a demonstration.

Two classmates were paired up as crossing guards and put into duty while the rest of us became the pedestrians. Each student had their turn putting on the Sam-Browne belt and carrying the flag as the guard. After completion of this exercise, we headed back to class.

The sergeant distributed honorary safety-patrol badges and a membership card imprinted with the School Safety Patrol pledge. My class was so excited, that those of us who didn't ride the bus, signed up as volunteers. We would be receiving training from the sixth-graders for eventual take over as guards. We were also trained to raise and lower the American flag, which was done daily by a member of the patrol.

PRINCIPAL LARRY JONES is pictured with Police Captain Schneider as the Lincoln Elementary "School-boy Patrol" receives an award as "Hoquiam's No. 1 Patrol Group." The award was earned for their outstanding service to their school and the community. Note that the boys are wearing the traditional Sam-Browne Safety Belts.

Principal Jones later recalled when one of the school-boy patrol students raced into his office. "There was a man going 100-miles an hour and wouldn't stop when I flagged him down," the student said. "I got a good look at the car; it was black and white with an eagle on the side."

Mr. Jones surmised that it was a State Patrolman's car, but praised the young man for his sharp eye and quick action.

LINCOLN ELEMENTARY (Circa 1970s)
Principal Larry Jones and Police Captain Schneider
With School-boy Patrol receiving "Hoquiam's No. 1 Patrol Group" award
(Courtesy of Larry R. Jones' collection)

IN THE 1965-66 school term, Girls Track and Field was added to all of Hoquiam's elementary schools. During one of the girl's practice sessions, the Lincoln Elementary team was training for a co-ed relay, but most of the boys refused to compete with them.

**EMERSON GRADE SCHOOL
1965 SONG QUEENS**
(Courtesy of the Polson Museum, Hoquiam, Wash., 2003.045.0020)

SONG-QUEEN TRYOUTS, 1965-1966
Story by: Diane Taylor

*"WE HAVE THE POWER. WE HAVE THE MIGHT.
We are the team that's going to score and win the game
with all our mighty-might-might!"*

MANY GRAMMER-SCHOOL GIRLS dreamed of being a Song Queen. Try-outs were open to everyone in the fifth grade.

Groups were formed, crepe-paper pom-poms handmade, and similar-colored skirts and blouses were worn. In our case, a neighbor overheard our group practicing and offered her left-over felt. She helped all four of us design our skirts, then sewed them together and taught us to handstitch musical notes to the skirt.

Wearing the outfits, we felt like real song queens and would practice for hours, hollering the yells while shaking the pom-poms to and fro. On try-out day, every group went on stage and performed their routines. The teachers and the PTA mothers determined the pick. None of my group made the cut, but we cherished our outfits. For Halloween that year we were song queens. We wore the skirts to some of the ballgames too and brought our poms-poms to cheer our team on.

HOQUIAM'S PUBLIC ELEMENTARY schools celebrated Valentine's Day. In the early years, the first and second graders drew Valentine cards in art class for their mothers and grandmothers. As time progressed, store-bought cards were introduced and distributed to all their classmates. This was done by grades one through six.

VALENTINE PARTY
EMERSON GRADE SCHOOL
Story by: Diane Taylor

YESTERDAY, Dean's Five 'n Dime on Simpson Avenue in Hoquiam displayed its new stock of Valentine cards, manufactured by Golden Books. The cards were sold separately or in a box of thirty-six. A booklet full of punch-out cards to assemble was also offered and provided many happy hours of fun just for you!

Each card had sweet and kind messages imprinted on them with a variety of characters, like elephants or rabbits, and lots of designs with Cupid. The really fancy ones were flocked with velveteen hearts and borders.

Every February, the grammar-school kids would pass out Valentine cards to each of their classmates and always one to the teacher.

The children made their own mailboxes out of paper sacks and beautified them with colorful crayon hearts. Each child printed their name on their mailbox, then hung it underneath the chalkboard for Valentine cards to be delivered in.

Each classroom was decorated with red and pink paper-hearts of all sizes and shapes. The bright hearts filled the windows and walls and were cleverly handmade by each youngster.

ON FEBRUARY 14TH, the whole school had an afternoon party. Every classroom was filled with delicious treats baked from home to eat. The school provided punch, ice-cream dixie cups, and party favors.

ELEMENTARY SCHOOL COMMONALITIES

> ## VALENTINE PARTY (CONTINUED)
> ## EMERSON GRADE SCHOOL
> Story by: Diane Taylor
>
> As each kid opened and saw all of the Valentine cards that were given to them, giggles and wide-eyed grins filled young hearts, swooning and looking across the room. So much joy and celebration were spent during the years of that special heartfelt day in that old-time school of yesterday.

VINTAGE VALENTINE CARDS
(Authors' collection)

1933 VALENTINE CARD
Made by Gladys, 6th Grade
Emerson Grade School
(Authors' collection)

HALLOWEEN WAS ANOTHER annual celebration for all of the grade schools, even the teachers and principals joined in with the festivities. One year Principal Krekow of Emerson Grade School appeared as a cowboy riding a horse. The head of a stuffed toy horse was sewn onto his shirt and a long bushy tail on the seat of his pants.

KAREN'S
Second-grade drawing
(Authors' collection)

KAREN, DIANE AND DOUG
HALLOWEEN DAY
EMERSON GRADE SCHOOL

ON HALLOWEEN DAY at Emerson, only morning classes were taught. Lunch was extended so students could dress in their costumes for the afternoon event. Those who lived close would go home, the others, including the school-bus kids, dressed in the lavatories. Volunteer mothers were on hand to help with their costumes.

Some students portrayed the personality of their costume character. A person dressed as a fairy princess might curtsy or grant a wish with her wand and several boys dressed as goblins or skeletons would jump out from hiding with a loud "boo!"

The Halloween parade began by one p.m., always starting with the kindergarteners, morning and afternoon classes combined for that day. Their teacher, who was also dressed up, led them through each classroom. Once the kindergarteners had completed their parade route and back in their seats, the first-graders were signaled to go. After they returned to their classroom, second-graders began their procession, and then third grade and so on.

AS THE MASQUERADERS serpentine down the hallway, laughter echoed. The children waiting in their seats were also poking fun with their classmates until the parade entered their room, then all attention was given to the Halloween characters.

AT LINCOLN ELEMENTARY, Principal Larry Jones, strumming his guitar, led the parade of teachers and students down the hallways and through the classrooms with a festive Halloween kickoff.

HALLOWEEN PARADE AT LINCOLN
(Courtesy of Larry R. Jones' collection)

CHAPTER 16
SCHOOL-RELATED ACTIVITIES

WITH THE CREATION of the Works Progress Administration in 1935, Hoquiam benefited with several public-works projects funded with federal money to boost the local economy and provide jobs for the unemployed. The Olympic Stadium, a vast arena to be used for multiple community and high-school events, was completed in 1938.

Pictured are Superintendent Crumpacker and Principal Rudie Oltman at the Olympic Stadium construction site. Rudie Oltman, Principal of both Hoquiam High School and Junior High, was the Chairman of the Park Board and key oversight of the building of the Olympic Stadium.

L TO R: Superintendent Crumpacker and Principal Rudie Oltman
(Courtesy of the Polson Museum, Hoquiam, Wash., 2008.016.0007)

THE FIRST Aberdeen vs Hoquiam Thanksgiving game at the Olympic Stadium was held on November 24, 1938. A pre-game dedication was performed by the Hoquiam High School marching band, song queens, yell kings, and majorettes.

1938 OLYMPIC STADIUM DEDICATION
HHS Song Queens, Marching Band, and Majorettes
(Courtesy of the Polson Museum, Hoquiam, Wash., 2010.036.0140)

IT WAS ESTIMATED that at least 2,000 spectators were seated in the visible wing of the bleachers. Note the unfinished roof to the right, pictured above.

1938 FIRST THANKSGIVING GAME AT THE OLYMPIC STADIUM
Aberdeen vs Hoquiam, November 24, 1938
(Courtesy of the Polson Museum, Hoquiam, Wash., 2002.071.0079)

**HOQUIAM HIGH SCHOOL MAJORETTES
DEDICATION OF THE OLYMPIC STADIUM (1938)**
(L to R): Mary Beth Root, Dorenne Worthley, Virginia Parsons
(Courtesy of the Polson Museum, Hoquiam, Wash., 1989.044.0034)

THE HOQUIAM HIGH SCHOOL majorettes' baton-twirling skills accentuated the marching band and were a highlight at games and parades. Baton twirling gained popularity in the late 1930s, and during this period, Hoquiam High School had introduced it as one of their after-school activities. It is unknown if this class continued through the 1940s, but outside organizations such as the Eagles and Elks sponsored classes where the girls marched in parades under their banner. Many of these same girls became the high school majorettes, leading their school's marching band.

Alice Norman Barbishe was one of Grays Harbor's well-known baton instructors, teaching in both Aberdeen and Hoquiam. In her youth, she won multiple championship trophies and even appeared on the Ted Mack TV show. In 1949, Alice's daughter, Lovey Ward, surpassed her mother's fame by winning the National and World Champion Baton Twirling award.

Lovey was also the head majorette for the Aberdeen Elks and the Aberdeen High School band in 1952 and 1953. During the annual Thanksgiving game in 1952, Aberdeen and Hoquiam combined their half-time formation. Lovey entertained the crowd with her twirling of two batons. As she threw them high into the air, she'd perform acrobatics, catching them under her leg and behind her back. In 1954, Lovey became the head majorette for the University of Washington and later at Stanford University in California. Through the years, she and her mother inspired many Harborite girls to become baton twirlers.

In the early 1960s, Alice taught baton lessons at the Eagles Hall to the Hoquiam grade-school and Hoquiam Junior High girls. The youngsters were grouped by age and size. Diane and Karen Taylor were among these twirlers.

During parades, the older twirlers, sixth grade and up, twirled as they marched. These majorettes represented the City of Hoquiam and the Hoquiam Eagles in parades throughout the state and also participated in competitions.

In the local parades, the younger majorettes, called the Eagle-ettes, carried their batons and followed the older twirlers like little toy soldiers. They sported similar colors: red stretch pants, white blouses and white tennis shoes with red pom-poms tied on. A red stretch band adorned their hair and a red ribbon hung from their collars.

LOVEY WARD
November 1952
(Courtesy of the Timberland Aberdeen Library, WA)

HOQUIAM EAGLES
Majorette uniform
(Fringed "V" later added)
(Authors' collection)

KAREN TAYLOR (1964-65)
7th grade, Hoquiam
McCleary Bear Festival Parade
(Authors' collection)

SCHOOL-RELATED ACTIVITIES

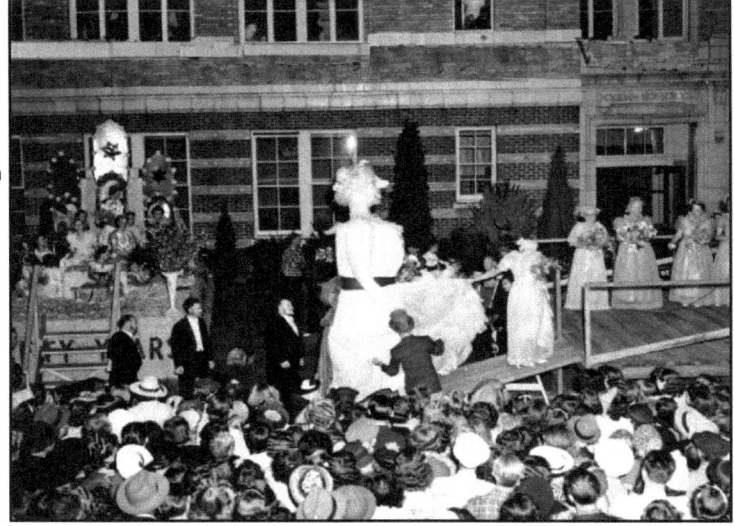

PAUL BUNYAN WEDDING PAUL BUNYAN JUBILEE 1939
(Courtesy of the Polson Museum, Hoquiam, 2002.049.0048 2002.49.050) ➡

THE 1939 PAUL BUNYAN JUBILEE lasted five days, but decorations and giant posters appeared months before. All the men were supposed to grow beards for a best-beard award given by the city.[1] Included in this five-day gala was a parade, an extravaganza at the Olympic Stadium, and Paul Bunyan's wedding to his sweetheart Pauline, staged at Hoquiam High School. Hoquiam High School girls, pictured on the float, were part of the celebration.

THE 50-YEAR CELEBRATION was a tribute of Hoquiam's growth through the wood industry. In 1889, Hoquiam's population had tripled from 400 to 1,500, which resulted in the city's incorporation the next year. That same year, November 1889, Washington became the 42nd state of the Union.

Excerpt from the 1939 *Washingtonian* newspaper:

HOQUIAM is honoring Paul Bunyan with a one-week festival, in fact is paying tribute to those who by their toil in forests and factories produce lumber and by producing it make it possible for Americans to say, "We are the best housed people in the world."

DURING THE JUBILEE, a gala at the Olympic Stadium, referred to as the "Spectacle" and titled: *They Live Again*, was presented on Thursday, Friday, and Saturday evenings as a colorful portrayal of Grays Harbor history. It was depicted in settings, commentary, action, music, and interpretive dance. It took months of preparation and $4,000 in expenses.

Twenty-four flood lights, twelve with colored rays, illuminated the 350-foot stage. The cast contained 750 Grays Harbor people, which included Hoquiam grade-school, junior-high, and high-school students. The script was written by Howard Hopkins, Hoquiam designer, and commentary by Frank Lamb. The Hilt Fireworks people of Seattle and Hoquiam residents: Howard Hopkins, Ruth Evanson and Lilah Williver directed the production. All of the costumes were designed by Hopkins and sewn by Hoquiam residents. The narrator was Arthur Lindsay of the KXRO radio station.

The action was staged on the lawn with a scenic backdrop one hundred-feet long and twenty-four feet high of the Olympic Mountains as seen from the head of the Hoquiam River. Plus, two other backdrops of equal size at each side depicting the foothills, waterfalls and the forests. The backdrops were designed by Hoquiam residents and built by the Hoquiam Manufacturing Company.

The Spectacle was performed in Episodes: the creation of the forest, the lives of the Native-Americans, Captain Robert Gray's arrival, Hoquiam's first pioneers: Johnny James, James Karr, and Edward Campbell, plus the creation of Hoquiam's FIRST SCHOOL, which featured Hoquiam grade-school children celebrating the advancement in education.

At the finale, the giant Paul Bunyan and his blue ox, Babe, slowly moved across the backdrops as symbols of "the might industry of the forest." [2]

GRAYS HARBOR VENEER COMPANY manufactured plywood, fruit and berry boxes, and miscellaneous containers for advertisement. Seeking new uses for their product, Laura Martin, a talented seamstress, volunteered to create garments on her treadle sewing machine.

Her daughter, Julia Martin, was the first Spruce Girl in 1929. She was later joined by her sister and four other young-women to promote Hoquiam's wood industry at various events. The Spruce Girl promotion occurred in the years 1929, 1932, 1939, and 1946, all with newly-styled wooden suits for their era.

The 1946 Spruce Girls were Hoquiam High Schoolers.

Spruce Girl, Julia Martin, in her 1929 wooden bathing suit, was pictured with Captain Matt Peasley of the ship, *Vigilant*. She was holding a giant wood-shaped foot, advertising the upcoming "Wood Week" celebration.[z] Smaller wooden feet were passed out at the event.

1929 "ORIGINAL" SPRUCE GIRLS IN THEIR "WOODEN" BATHING SUITS
(Courtesy of the Polson Museum
Hoquiam, Wash)

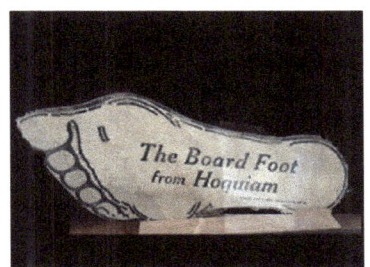

THE BOARD FOOT
1929 Wood Week
(Courtesy of the Polson Museum. Hoquiam, Wash)

In the early 1930s, the Hoquiam High School Domestic-Science Department designed and sewed veneer garments and bathing suits. They were featured in a 1930s *National Geographic* magazine. These same garments may have been used by the 1932 Spruce Girls.

---

[z] Pictured on Page 67 of *On the Harbor, From Black Friday to Nirvana* by John C. Hughes and Ryan Teague Beckwith, published 2005, 2012, Stephens Press, L.L.C, Las Vegas, NV.)

**HOQUIAM HIGH SCHOOL DOMESTIC-SCIENCE DEPARTMENT
WEARING SITKA SPRUCE VENEER CLOTHING
NATIONAL GEOGRAPHIC MAGAZINE (Circa 1930s)**

(Courtesy of the Polson Museum, Hoquiam, Wash., 2017.078.0018)

THE ABOVE PICTURE and article appeared in a 1930's "*National Geographic:*"

HOQUIAM GIRLS WITH WOODEN DRESSES MIGHT POSE AS TREE NYMPHS

From Sitka spruce veneer, an eightieth of an inch thick, the high school domestic-science department fashions fancy costumes and bathing suits. Transparent sheets of fir are used as stationery, and at Tenino, a bank has printed currency on wood.

In the 1946 "wood" promotion, Hoquiam High School girls were chosen to be the Spruce Girls. A short film of them at Lake Quinault was used as advertisement for the Grays Harbor lumber industry and distributed to theaters nationwide.

1946 SPRUCE GIRLS
(Courtesy of the Polson Museum, Hoquiam, Wash.,
2022.062.0047)

HOQUIAM HIGH SCHOOLER'S: Dorothy Iroala, Mary Viducick, Gloria Byrnes, Betty Poust, Lois Hart, Edith Sandberg, Doris Lucas, Arlene Lukes, and Marilyn Coleman.

1946 SPRUCE GIRL BATHING SUIT
(Courtesy of the Polson Museum
Hoquiam, Wash)

**1902 YMCA
THREE STORY, HIP ROOFED
SIXTH AND "J" STREET**
(Courtesy of the Polson Museum, Hoquiam, Wash., 2001.018.0023)

THE FIRST GRAYS HARBOR Y.M.C.A.[aa] was formed in Hoquiam in 1902 on Sixth and J Streets. Central No. 1 was built the next year, but for classrooms only. The new YMCA, with its large multi-purpose room and gym, became an extension of the school, especially in the beginning for indoor sports, exercising, and school events.

**1906 YMCA SCHOOL PARTY
YMCA Multi-purpose Room**
(Courtesy of the Polson Museum, Hoquiam, Wash., 2001.095.0422)

[aa] Y.M.C.A.: Young Men's Christian Association.

SCHOOL-RELATED ACTIVITIES

1911 EXERCISE CLASS YMCA GYM
(Courtesy of the Polson Museum, Hoquiam,
Wash., 2001.095.0423)

**FIRST YMCA
BASKETBALL CHAMPS
(1911-1912)
Coach Oscar Lovgren
Left to Right:** Lester Hanson,
Ernest Bemis, Bob Gorden,
Guy Narrance.
(Seated) Bob Clark, George
Palmer and John Marrs
(Authors' collection)

1937 YMCA BASKETBALL TEAM
(Courtesy of the Polson Museum,
Hoquiam, Wash., 1982.044.0006)

During the Depression years, 1930-1939, each member of the 1937 YMCA Basketball team was sponsored by Hoquiam businesses: Al Lawrence Service, Prichard Hardware, F.G. Foster, Griffen Service, and Root Paint Company.

THE GRAND CENTRAL Public Market building, erected in 1923 on Seventh and K Streets, had been transformed five times. After the Market's closure, the second tenant was the Totem Grocery, its third was one of the two original Boeing plants, and fourth was the Motor Buggy Trailer Supply Company. When the Motor Buggy Trailer Supply Company closed, the building later became the new location for Hoquiam's YMCA in the early 1960s.

**GRAND CENTRAL PUBLIC MARKET (Circa 1928)
CONVERTED INTO THE YMCA IN THE EARLY 1960s**
(Courtesy of the Polson Museum, Hoquiam, Wash., 2006.058.0080)

**YMCA BUS TRIP TO OLYMPIA
FOR STUDENT GOVERNMENT DAY
(Circa 1962)**

Courtesy of the Polson Museum, Hoquiam, Wash.
Bus trip: 2001.095.0152
Dance: 2001.095.0147

1962 YMCA SWEETHEART DANCE

**YMCA ACTIVITIES
(Circa 1960s)**
Courtesy of the Polson Museum,
Hoquiam, Wash.
**2001.096.0001
2001.095.0016
2001.095.0101**

HOQUIAM AQUATIC Center was built in 1963 adjacent to the YMCA on K Street. Swim classes and after-school swim meets were integrated into the school curriculum.

ACQUATIC CENTER (Circa 1960s)
(Courtesy of the Polson Museum, Hoquiam, Wash.,
2001.095.0030)

CHAPTER 17
THE HOQUIAM PUBLIC LIBRARY

HOQUIAM CARNEGIE LIBRARY
(Courtesy of the Polson Museum, Hoquiam, Wash., 2021.023.0208)

IN 1907, FRANK LAMB[bb] spearheaded the movement for a free public library for the city of Hoquiam. The next year,1908, the city adopted the resolution with a board of trustees, which elected Frank Lamb as President, and provided an appropriation of $2,500 per year for the library's operation. One of Mr. Lamb's first acts was contacting Andrew Carnegie's secretary, James Bertram, with a request of $25,000 to build a new library. In the interim, a house had been converted into the library. Miss Maud Macpherson of Watertown, Wisconsin was hired as Hoquiam's first librarian.

MAY 1910, Hoquiam was gifted $20,000 from the Andrew Carnegie library fund. The architectural firm of Claude and Starck, Madison, Wisconsin, was selected. Miss Macpherson, Hoquiam's librarian, had worked in the Evansville, Wisconsin Public Library, which was designed by the same architectural firm.

[bb] Frank Lamb was the founder of the Hoquiam Machine Works and Lamb Timber Company, later renamed Lamb-Grays Harbor Company. He served as the President of the Library board until his passing in 1951.

It was noted that she had some input with the final selection. It was also noted that Mr. Claude was a close friend to architects Louis Sullivan and Frank Lloyd Wright. His designs were influenced by these two men.

With its low-pitched roof and extended, sheltering eaves, and low-to-the-ground design, the Hoquiam Library was described as a Prairie-style. Not only was the design uncommon to the Northwest, it was unlike most of the other Carnegie libraries. [1]

Local contractor, Fred Knack[cc], was hired as the builder and Frank Lamb was the supervising architect. On August 25, 1911, in the presence of 400 people, the library was dedicated and presented by Frank Lamb to the city on behalf of Andrew Carnegie.[2] The Hoquiam Woman's club gifted a tall mahogany clock. Later, a cast bronze tablet was placed above the upstairs fireplace stating:

> *"This building is the gift of Andrew Carnegie, maintained by the City of Hoquiam."*

SINCE ITS OPENING, Hoquiam's library became a cornerstone for the young and old alike. Prior to the introduction of the television, reading was one of the favorite pastimes. A rainy-day outing to find that special book and to stay awhile to read, was a must.

All of the elementary schools planned field trips to the library. Once there, they would meet the librarian and get a guided tour of how to search for books and services offered. Some would sign up for a library card and pick out books for an upcoming book report. High school students frequented too.

**Fairyland Exhibit:
"Mary, Mary Quite Contrary"**
(Hoquiam Public Library, Scrapbook archives)

FOR THIRTY-TWO YEARS, 1933-1965, Miss Marion Taft manned the helm of the Hoquiam Library. In addition to her friendly smile and kind nature, she organized children's book clubs, summer reading programs, and exhibits such as the Fairyland display. She made reading fun.

[cc] Father to Clara Knack Dooley, author of *School Days' 1900*.

HOQUIAM PUBLIC LIBRARY "UPSTAIRS INTERIOR"
(Circa 1940s)
(Courtesy of the Hoquiam Public Library, Scrapbook archives)

**HOQUIAM PUBLIC LIBRARY "CHILDREN'S ROOM"
DOWNSTAIRS** (Circa 1940s)
(Courtesy of the Hoquiam Public Library, Scrapbook archives)

NOVEMBER 16, 1943, with WWII at its height, head librarian Miss Marion Taft and her staff hosted a special event in observance of "National Book Week." The theme of their event, "Build the Future with Books," was highlighted by attention-grabbing displays, showcased in the downstairs children's room of the library.

Upon entry into the Children's Library, seventy-five colorful new books for all ages were displayed for the youngsters to browse and check out before being officially cataloged and put into circulation. There were also three decorated tables for the children to view, each with their own flavor and the same beginning message: "Build the Future with Books About..."

Table One: "About our Homes." Table Two: "About our Nation." Table Three: "About the World." Books and artifacts that pertained to these themes were exhibited. The one that stood above them all, was the dollhouse on table one, decorated in a Victorian style. This dollhouse became so popular that it converted into a permanent fixture in the children's library for the next twenty-two years.

The dollhouse was built by Joe Wilson, pattern maker at Lamb's, and was decorated by Miss Taft with the assistance of her sister, Mrs. Frances Jukes, and library assistants, Miss Winifred Walden and Miss Armyn Goodwin. The miniature furnishings had been collected by Miss Taft over the years. Every room was decorated with precise detail.

HOQUIAM PUBLIC LIBRARY "CHILDREN'S ROOM" ORIGINAL DOLLHOUSE (1943)
(Hoquiam Public Library, Scrapbook archives)

The original dollhouse, pictured, remained with the library until Miss Taft's retirement in 1965. It was then gifted to her niece.

In 1995, thirty years after her retirement, Miss Taft, now age ninety-five, set out on a mission to build another dollhouse for the Hoquiam Public Library. With the aid of her gardener, Jeanie Scott, they accomplished her goal.

Original 1943 Dollhouse

The children's library room was gone, but the new dollhouse found a home upstairs. Miss Taft designed and decorated every room with the same precision as the original dollhouse.

New 1995 Dollhouse

RECAP, BIOS, AND REFERENCES

CHAPTER 18
RECAP
THE EVOLUTION OF HOQUIAM'S SCHOOLS

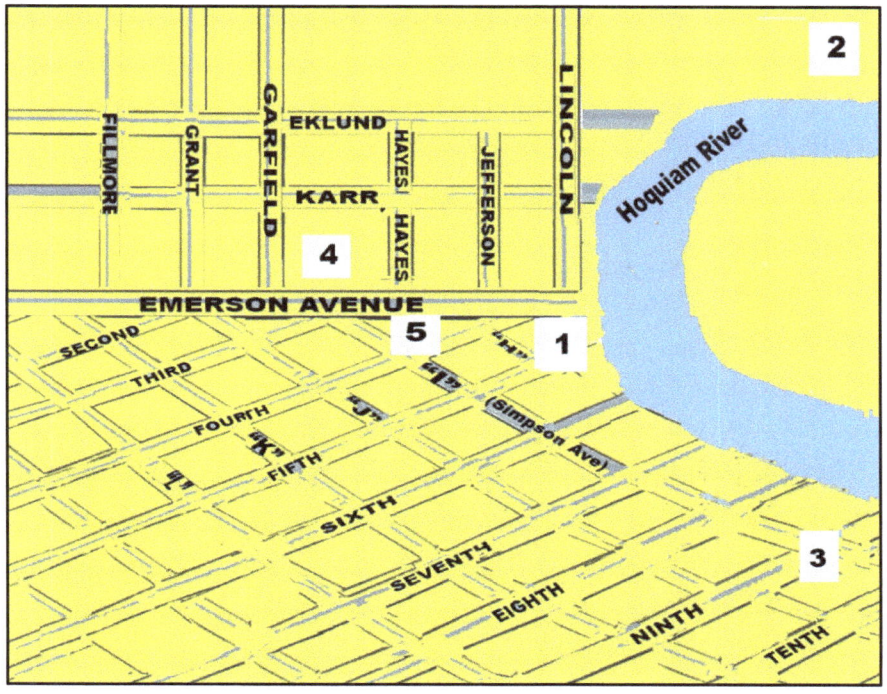

MAP OF HOQUIAM'S EARLY SCHOOLS (1873-1903)
(Authors' collection)

#1 – **FIRST "OFFICIAL" SCHOOL, 1873-1880,** Fifth and "H" Streets.

#2 – **SECOND SCHOOL, 1880-1882,** later site of EK Wood Sawmill.

#3 – **STEVENS SCHOOL 1882-1903,** Ninth and "I" Streets.

#4 – **HOQUIAM PUBLIC SCHOOL (MCKINLEY)**, **1892,** renamed to MCKINLEY IN **1897.** Emerson Ave. and Garfield Street.

#5 – **CENTRAL NO. 1, 1903, located in the** "I" Street, Emerson Avenue, and Fourth Street triangle.

#1 – **FIRST "OFFICIAL" SCHOOL, 1873-1880,** Fifth and "H" Streets, Hoquiam. School District No. #5.
- ❖ Five children of available age were required to establish a school. Olive Karr (7), Beatrice Karr (6), Elk Karr (4), Rose Agnes Campbell (9), and Laura Campbell (4) were the first students.
- ❖ Johnny James' second abandoned cabin was used as the first school.
- ❖ In operation six years.
- ❖ The site was the later location of the Hoquiam Sash and Door Co. on Fifth and "H" Streets.

#2 – **SECOND SCHOOL, 1880-1882,** replaced the first school building. School District #5

- ❖ Erected upstream after the first school #1 began to deteriorate.
- ❖ Additional students were added.
- ❖ This site later became the location of the E.K. Wood Sawmill.

#3 – **STEVENS SCHOOL 1882-1903,** Ninth and "I" Street, Hoquiam.

- ❖ Built in 1882.
- ❖ Named after Territorial Governor Isaac Stevens.
- ❖ By 1884, Hoquiam had grown in territory and pupils and qualified as its own school district, forming district no. #28.
- ❖ All grades, one through ten, were taught here.
- ❖ After completion of McKinley in 1892, "sixth grade" only was taught at Stevens for another decade.

STEVENS SCHOOL
(Courtesy of Larry Jones' collection)

#4 – HOQUIAM PUBLIC SCHOOL (MCKINLEY), 1892, renamed to McKinley in 1897. Emerson Avenue and Garfield Street.

- ❖ Named after President McKinley in 1897.
- ❖ All primary and intermediate classes, one through eight, except for sixth grade, were taught on the first and second floors.
- ❖ High school, ninth and tenth, were taught on the third floor.
- ❖ 1902, Dr. Warde added eleventh-grade courses.

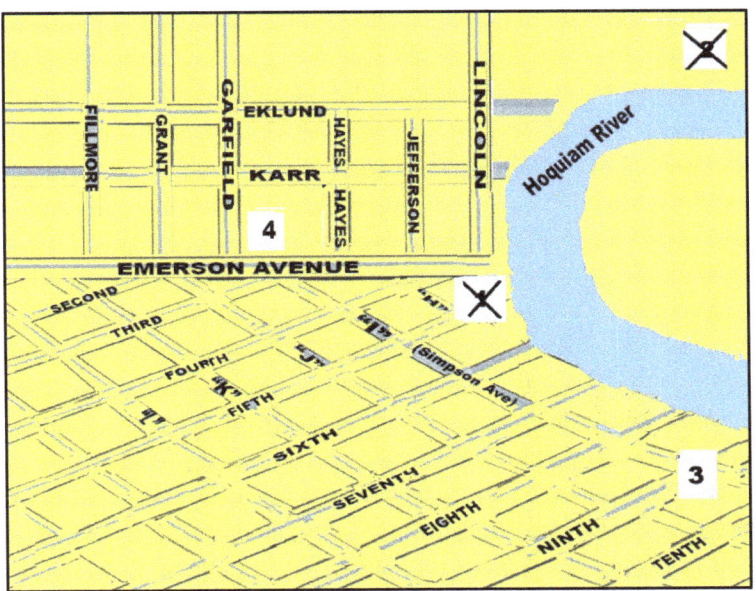

1892-1903 MAP OF HOQUIAM SCHOOLS
(Authors' collection)

1892 - JUNE 1903, TWO Hoquiam Public Schools were in operation:

(#3) STEVENS SCHOOL
- ❖ Sixth grade ONLY.

(#4) MCKINLEY
- ❖ Grades one through fifth.
- ❖ Grades seventh through eleventh

#5 – CENTRAL NO. 1, BUILT IN 1903 on the "I" Street, Emerson Avenue, and Fourth Street triangle. Also referred to as School #5.

- ❖ The sixth graders were transferred from Stevens to McKinley. Stevens School, thereafter, was used for miscellaneous events.
- ❖ Seventh and eighth graders were transferred from McKinley to Central No. 1's first-floor classrooms.[1]
- ❖ Twelfth grade courses were added under Professor Burkhead's administration.
- ❖ Ninth through twelfth graders were transferred from McKinley to Central No. 1's second-floor plus two basement classrooms.

SEPTEMBER 1903 - 1907, TWO Hoquiam Public Schools were in operation.

(#4) MCKINLEY ELEMENTARY
- ❖ McKinley became an elementary school only.
- ❖ Grades one through sixth.

(#5) CENTRAL NO. 1
- ❖ Grades seventh through twelfth.

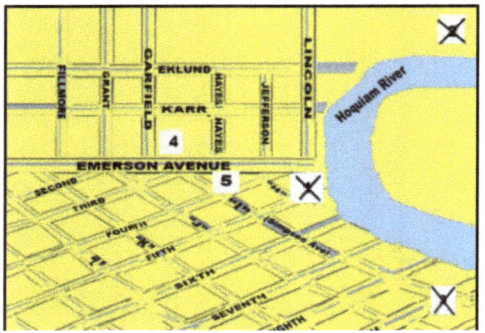

SEPTEMBER 1903 MAP OF HOQUIAM SCHOOLS
(Authors' collection)

CENTRAL NO. 1 MCKINLEY IN THE BACKGROUND
(Courtesy of the Polson Museum, Hoquiam, Wash.
2014.011.0007)

#6 – LINCOLN ELEMENTARY, BUILT IN 1907, OPENED IN 1908, on Lincoln Avenue, Hoquiam, Washington.

- ❖ Grades one through sixth for the children in the northern section of town.
- ❖ Grays Harbor City School was closed and many of its students transferred to Lincoln.
- ❖ Its school colors were red and black, and their mascot was Abraham Lincoln. They were called the "Abes."

#7 – WASHINGTON SCHOOL OPENED IN 1908 on "I" Street (later renamed Simpson Avenue), Hoquiam, Washington, across the river.

- ❖ Grades one through eight for the children living across the Hoquiam River.
- ❖ Its school colors were blue and gold and the team's name was the Bulldogs.

SEPTEMBER 1910, FOUR Hoquiam Public Schools were in operation.

(Courtesy of the Polson Museum, Hoquiam, Wash., 2021.023.0253)

(#4) MCKINLEY ELEMENTARY
- ❖ One through sixth grade.

(#5) CENTRAL NO. 1
- ❖ Grades seventh through twelfth.

(#6) LINCOLN ELEMENTARY
- ❖ One through sixth grade.

(#7) WASHINGTON SCHOOL
- ❖ One through eighth grade.

WITH THE BUILDING of the new high school in 1913-1914, McKinley had to be moved several feet to accommodate. In her prime, she was the pride of the town, standing tall like a sentinel on an island of her own. Now she would be crowded next to a brick-and-mortar temple, making her a relic of the past.

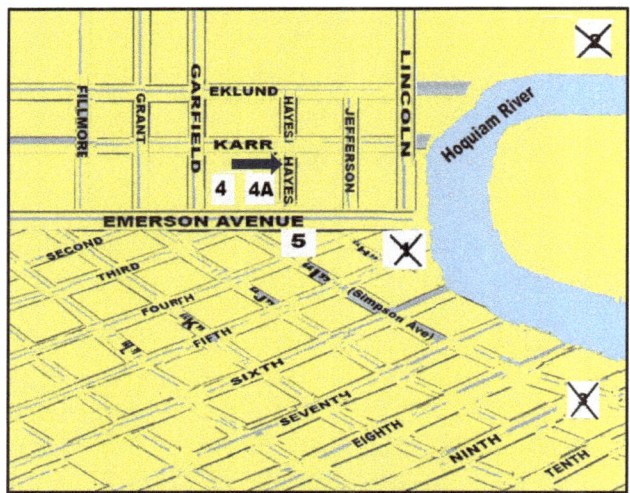

1913 MAP OF HOQUIAM SCHOOLS
MCKINLEY #4 moved a few feet #4A
(Authors' collection)

**1914 NEW HOQUIAM HIGH SCHOOL NEXT TO
MCKINLEY after it was moved**
(Courtesy of the Polson Museum, Hoquiam, Wash.
1985.062.0001)

#8 – HOQUIAM HIGH SCHOOL, BUILT 1913-1914. Emerson Avenue and Garfield.

- ❖ 1913-1914, the new high school was completed. (#8)
- ❖ High School started September 1914.
- ❖ Seventh through ninth grade remained at Central No. 1. (#5)
- ❖ First through sixth grade remained at McKinley. (#4A)

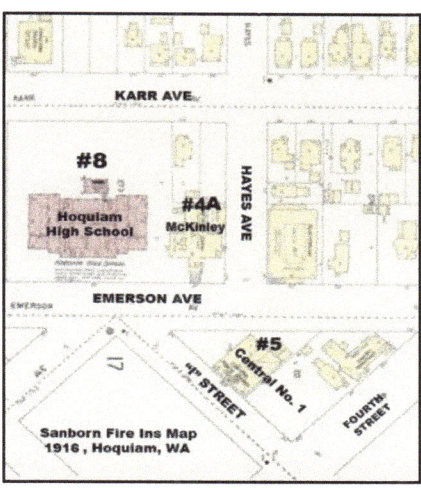

1916 SANBORN FIRE INS. MAP

1913-14 NEW "HOQUIAM HIGH SCHOOL" (#8) IN THE BACKGROUND

CENTRAL SCHOOL NO 1 (#5) IN FOREGROUND
("I" Street, Emerson Avenue and Fourth Street)

(Courtesy of the Polson Museum, Hoquiam, Wash., 2003.006.0019)

(MCKINLEY, NOW MOVED, CAN NO LONGER BE VIEWED FROM THIS ANGLE. SEE PREVIOUS PICTURE ON PAGE 204)

IN 1918, FIVE Hoquiam Public Schools were in operation. Lincoln and Washington are not pictured.

- (#4A) MCKINLEY ELEMENTARY (1892)
- (#5) CENTRAL NO. 1 (1903)
- (#6) LINCOLN ELEMENTARY (Built 1907, Opened 1908)
- (#7) WASHINGTON SCHOOL (1908)
- (#8) HOQUIAM HIGH SCHOOL (Built 1913-1914, Opened 1914)

#X - SCHOOLS #1, #2, and #3 (Stevens) razed or out of commission.

HOQUIAM PUBLIC SCHOOLS (1918)
(Courtesy of the Polson Museum, Hoquiam, Wash., 2011.065.3466)

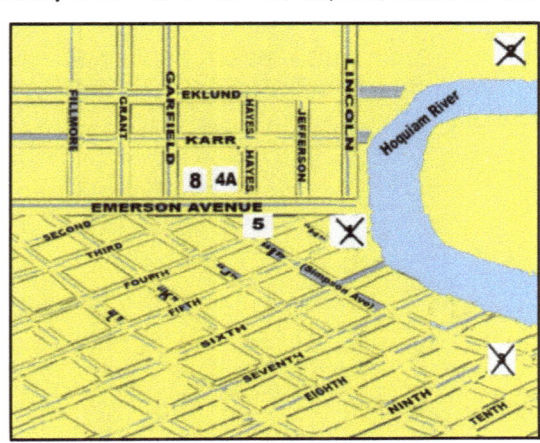

IN 1922, EMERSON ELEMENTARY was added to Hoquiam's School District #28.

EMERSON GRADE SCHOOL
(Courtesy of Polson Museum archives)

#9 – EMERSON ELEMENTARY (1922)

- Named after George H. Emerson, who was often called the "Father of Hoquiam."
- Grades one through sixth for the children in the west end of town.
- Located on Emerson Avenue and Adams.
- Its school colors were green and white and team name, the Tigers.

IN 1926, HOQUIAM JR HIGH AND CENTRAL NO. 2 were added to Hoquiam's School District #28.

#10 – HOQUIAM "JR" HIGH, (1926) Emerson Ave.
- To make room for two new schools (Hoquiam Jr. High and Central No. 2), **Hayes Avenue was realigned** to start at Karr.
- McKinley (#4A) was demolished.
- By the mid-1930s, Superintendent's office was in the front, arched half-dome window on the second floor.[dd]
- Per 1927 freshman notes (*Hesperian*), ninth grade classes had been moved to the new Junior High School building #10.

[dd] Per interview with Ray Connell, authors' cousin

(#10) NEW HOQUIAM JR. HIGH (1926)
Built on OLD MCKINLEY site
(Courtesy of the Polson Museum, Hoquiam,
Wash.2013.046.0041)

#11 – CENTRAL NO. 2 ELEMENTARY (1926) Emerson Ave and Jefferson.

- ❖ McKinley School (#4A) remained in operation through the end of school term 1924 or so.
- ❖ In 1925, McKinley was razed and Central No. 2 and Hoquiam Jr. High School were built.
- ❖ Central No. 2 (#11) replaced McKinley (#4A) for elementary students, one through six, living in the central portion of town.
- ❖ One of Hoquiam's first public-school kindergartens was added in the 1940s at Central No 2.

(#11) CENTRAL NO. 2 (1926)
(Courtesy of the Polson Museum, Hoquiam, Wash.,2013.046.0040)

IN 1926, SEVEN Hoquiam Public Schools were in operation:

(#5)   CENTRAL NO. 1 (1903)
(#6)   LINCOLN ELEMENTARY (Built 1907, Opened 1908)
(#7)   WASHINGTON SCHOOL (1908)
(#8)   HOQUIAM HIGH SCHOOL (Built 1913-1914, Opened 1914)
(#9)   EMERSON ELEMENTARY (1922)
(#10) HOQUIAM "JR" HIGH (1926). **Built on old McKinley site.**
(#11) CENTRAL NO. 2 ELEMENTARY (1926). Next to the NEW Junior High school.

(#4A) MCKINLEY DEMOLISHED, 1926. **Hayes Ave was realigned. Hayes Avenue used to start at Emerson Avenue.**
(#X) SCHOOLS #1, #2, and #3 (Stevens) razed or out of commission.

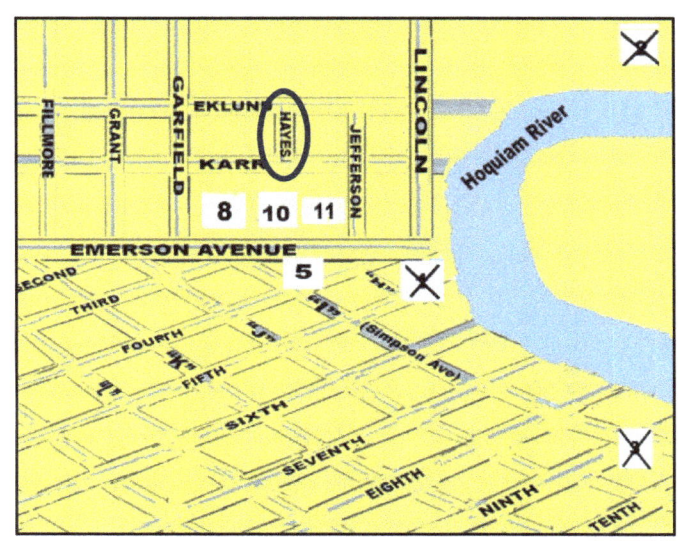

1926 MAP OF HOQUIAM SCHOOLS
MCKINLEY was demolished, HAYES AVENUE was realigned
#10 HOQUIAM JR. HIGH (1926)
#11 CENTRAL NO. 2 (1926)
(Authors' collection)

HOQUIAM HIGH AND JUNIOR HIGH SCHOOL COMPOUND, (Circa 1927)
(Courtesy of Jones Photo Historical Collection #L400274_1)

BASED ON THE interview of Monroe Kosoff and Harold Erickson, Hoquiam High School graduates, 1930s. Central No. 1 (#5), located in the triangle across the street from the high school, was still being used for seventh and eighth-grade classes.

> Interview:
> *"Where was the high school building?"*
> Answer by Mr. Erickson: *"It was on Emerson. Central school was in the triangle by the high school. No crossing guard was posted, so H.S. students would pull a rope across between two telephone poles for central kids to cross. Mr. Erickson's uncle ran into the rope and broke his windshield but didn't hit a kid!"* (Hoquiam High School, 100 Years of Grizzly Pride! 1891-1991, page 29, Grizzly Trivia from the 30s by David Quigg.) ee

---

ee Monroe Kosoff and Harold Erickson interview.

#12 – **NEW GYM AND CLASSROOMS**, were built behind the high school (1936). Karr Ave and Garfield.

- After the 1929 stock market crash, Superintendent Crumpacker kept the school district afloat on a "cash" basis.[ff]
- 1936, a new gym and classrooms were added.
- Crumpacker also doubled the athletic and educational studies.
- The Hesperian subscribed a dedication to "Superintendent Crumpacker" for taking the school through the Depression, adding that a "new" gym and entire wing of classrooms were added in 1936.

NEW BUILDING ADDED #12, (1936)
Behind High School
(Courtesy of the Polson Museum, Hoquiam, Wash., 2007.011.0007)

1936 MAP OF HOQUIAM SCHOOLS
New Gym and Classrooms, #12
(Authors' collection)

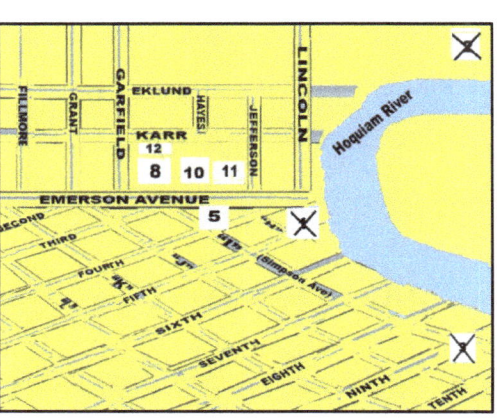

[ff] Hoquiam High School 1891-1991 Pamphlet, page 13, 1936.

HOQUIAM PUBLIC SCHOOLS COMPOUND
(Courtesy of the Polson Museum, Hoquiam, Wash.2002.012.0009)

IN 1936, SIX Hoquiam Public Schools were in operation:
(Note: #12 HHS Gym and classroom wing were part of Hoquiam High School and "not" added into this number.)

(#5) CENTRAL NO. 1 (1903) GONE BY THE LATE 1930S
(#6) LINCOLN ELEMENTARY (Built 1907, Opened 1908)
(#7) WASHINGTON SCHOOL (1908)
(#8) HOQUIAM HIGH SCHOOL (Built 1913-1914, Opened 1914)
(#9) EMERSON ELEMENTARY (1922)
(#10) HOQUIAM "JR" HIGH (1926). Built on old McKinley site.
(#11) CENTRAL NO. 2 ELEMENTARY (1926)
(#12) HHS GYM AND NEW WING OF CLASSROOMS (1936)

IN 1953, Central No. 3 Elementary was added to Hoquiam's School District #28. Central No. 1 was now gone.

#13 – CENTRAL NO. 3, Simpson Avenue, Hoquiam, WA (1953)

- New larger elementary school.
- Central No. 2 was converted into Junior and Senior High school use.
- Its school colors were blue and white and team name, the Bears.

**CENTRAL NO. 3
CENTRAL ELEMENTARY (1953)
Replaced Central No. 2**
(Courtesy of the Polson Museum, Hoquiam, Wash., 2017.017.0013)

IN 1953, SEVEN Hoquiam Public Schools were in operation:

(#6)   LINCOLN ELEMENTARY (Built 1907, Opened 1908)
(#7)   WASHINGTON SCHOOL (1908)
(#8)   HOQUIAM HIGH SCHOOL (Built 1913-1914, Opened 1914)
(#9)   EMERSON ELEMENTARY (1922)
(#10) HOQUIAM "JR" HIGH (1926). Built on old McKinley site.
(#11) CENTRAL NO. 2 (1926). Next to NEW Junior High.
(#13) CENTRAL NO. 3 (1953)

(#12) **HHS GYM AND NEW WING OF CLASSROOMS (1936), part of the high school.**
(#5)   **CENTRAL NO. 1 (1903) GONE.**

AFTER A MAJOR remodeling of Central No. 2 in 1956, it was quickly realized that they had already outgrown the space for the existing 1,500 headcount.[2]

CHAPTER 19
RECAP
CENTRAL SCHOOLS 1,2,3

CENTRAL NO. 1 (1903)
(Courtesy of the Polson Museum, Hoquiam, Wash.,1977.028.0010)

CENTRAL NO. 1, 1903, "I" Street, Emerson Ave. and Fourth Street triangle.
- Completed in 1903.
- Seventh and eighth grades, were moved from McKinley to the first floor of **Central No. 1**.
- High school, ninth through twelfth grades, were moved from McKinley to **Central No. 1** and occupied the second floor, plus several rooms in the basement.
- When the new high school was built in 1914, seventh, eighth and ninth grades remained at **Central No. 1.**
- When Hoquiam Jr High was completed in **1926,** only ninth graders moved into the new building. Seventh and eighth grade classes remained at **Central No. 1**. These assumptions are based on the 1935 Hesperian (Freshman notes), and D. Taylor's interview with a woman who attended Central No. 1 in the 1930s.
- Central No. 1 was razed or possibly moved **by the mid-1930s.**

CENTRAL NO. 2 (1926)
(Courtesy of the Polson Museum, Hoquiam, Wash.,2013.046.0040)

CENTRAL NO. 2, (1926), Emerson Ave and Jefferson.

- Est. 1925, McKinley was razed and **Central No. 2** and Hoquiam Junior High were completed in 1926.
- **Central No. 2** replaced McKinley. All elementary students, one through six grades, living in the central portion of town, attended this school.
- One of the first kindergartens of the Hoquiam public school system was taught at Central No. 2 in the 1940s.
- Seventh and eighth grades remained at Central No. 1 through the early 1930s.
- Ninth graders were later put into the Hoquiam Jr. building, which also housed the superintendent.
- With the building of Central No. 3, in 1953, **Central No. 2** was converted for the Hoquiam Junior and Senior High school use.
- After a major remodeling of Central No. 2 in 1956, it was quickly realized that they had already outgrown the space for the existing 1,500 headcount.[1]

DURING THE 1950's, many of the aging schools needed renovation or demolition to prepare for the baby-boomer population flooding the schools. Rebuilds or new additions would be streamlined with one-story, modernized structures.

In 1951, the Hoquiam School Board directors developed a long-range plan for the building needs of all of the schools in their district. The first in line was a new and larger **Central Elementary, Central No. 3**, for the students living in the central portion of town.

**CENTRAL NO. 3
ELEMENTARY SCHOOL**
(Replaced Central No. 2)
(Courtesy of the Polson Museum, Hoquiam, Wash., 2017.017.0013)

CENTRAL NO. 3, (Built 1953) Simpson Avenue, Hoquiam.

- **Central No. 3** was built in 1953, across the street and kitty corner from the old Central No. 1 triangle site.
- All kindergarten and elementary students in the central portion of Hoquiam were transferred from Central No. 2 to **Central No. 3**.

LARRY R. JONES
BIO

LARRY R. JONES WAS A LEADER and an all-American sports fan at an early age. When the Jones' family arrived to Aberdeen, Washington from Arizona in 1944, Larry was nine-years-old. From age nine to thirteen, he worked as a newspaper boy. At age twelve, he sold the most newspaper subscriptions and won a trip by train to San Francisco to see a 49er's game, which he traveled to on his own.

Larry attended Stevens Elementary School in Aberdeen and played with the South Aberdeen baseball team, near his home, at Pioneer Park. It was here where he perfected every aspect of the sport: shagging, chasing, and racing to catch fly balls in the outfield, which made him a shoe-in for the Class-A baseball team at Weatherwax High School. He played on the team all three years. He also participated in basketball for two years, the Athletic Club three years, and assisted with the Squad-B football team as a manager in his sophomore year.

Weatherwax Baseball Team
Larry R. Jones, back row, **seventh from left**
(Black sleeves, arms crossed)

In addition to sports, Larry expanded into leader-ship roles. First, as the junior class president, an elected position. The next year as a senior, he served on the Senate and was the president of the Boys' Federation. The Senate was the main governing body of the school and composed of seven members of the "Board of

Board of Control Senate Members
Larry R. Jones, first from left

Control," plus one representative from each homeroom, and delegates from different organizations of the school. All transactions passed in the Senate were governed by a constitution and set rules of procedures. The senators were responsible for passing bills, making appropriations, discussing problems and projects for the betterment of the school. As the Boys' Federation president, Larry was responsible for heading up support committees. Some of their offsite activities included: selling programs and concessions, sponsoring contests, and taking care of traffic at all games. His final contribution was when he was chosen to be the faculty commencement speaker at his 1953 high-school graduation.

From high school, he attended Grays Harbor College earning his associate degree. During his high school and early college years, he worked as a bellhop at the Mork Hotel. In 1957, he graduated from Western Washington University with a teaching degree. At both of these institutions, he was the catcher for their baseball teams.

With his degree in hand, he returned to Grays Harbor and secured a position at Lincoln Elementary School in Hoquiam, where he taught sixth grade for the next three years, through the end of the school term 1960. He then enrolled at the University of Oregon in Eugene for postgraduate studies. In the fall of 1960, he was hired by Emerson Elementary School as both the sixth-grade teacher of math, history, and science, and as the athletic director. His sixth-grade teaching was shared with Mrs. Lewis, where she handled the English, literature, music, and health and the other academics while he devoted part of his time to his athletic responsibilities, plus taught boys and girls PE. During school breaks, he attended the University of Oregon again and continued this schedule until 1962. This same year, he was approached and encouraged by his mentor, Mr. Krekow, the Emerson principal, to apply for the principal vacancy at Lincoln Elementary School, which proved to be the right fit. For the next fourteen years, September 1963 through June 1977, he set up office in the old 1907 school basement and thrived as Lincoln's principal. He stated that these years at Lincoln hold some of his fondest memories.

In 1978, he was transferred to Emerson Elementary as the principal, where he worked for one year. At Emerson, he created a detailed PTO handbook for both parents and teachers with a membership drive, hoping to encourage parent participation and attendance at the monthly meetings.

Later, Larry accepted the position as Central Elementary School's principal, which he held for the next five years, through the end of school term

1986. Without missing a beat, he headed to the University of Washington for more postgraduate courses through the years 1986, 1987, and 1988. During this period, he was promoted to assistant superintendent, handling all the budgets, contracts, food programs, and various administrative staff including the bus drivers and custodians. He held this position for the next ten years until his retirement in 1997, which ended his forty-year career with the Hoquiam School District.

His early years as a teacher, he coached both boy and girl's teams. Through all of his years in Hoquiam, he also officiated sports, especially baseball, where he umpired the Hoquiam, Aberdeen, and Grays Harbor College games. Larry and Don Holmlund wrote the first Title I Program for Hoquiam. He also headed the team that implemented the Title IX Program for girls in the Hoquiam schools.

Larry joined the Navy Reserve in high school, continued through college and through his time as a teacher at Lincoln Elementary, a total of eight years. The weekly meetings centered around classroom studies and periodic marching and gun drills. Yearly trips to San Diego, for two weeks, afforded him hands-on boat training at sea.

In retirement, he geared up his leadership skills as an active member and committee organizer for various community clubs, organizations, and sporting events throughout Grays Harbor County. He also served as the Lions Club President. In addition to regular supported activities throughout the year, he's been a key component with the annual rain derby and Loggers' Playday events.

**ASSISTANT SUPERINTENDENT
LARRY R. JONES**
(Courtesy of Larry R. Jones' collection)

ABOUT THE AUTHORS

Diane and Karen Taylor's Grays Harbor roots span back to the 1880's. Their father, a historian and steam-artifact collector, wrote throughout his life for local newspapers and historical magazines. His love of history and writing was passed down to his daughters. When collaborating on a project, the sisters use their pen name, DK Taylor.

Diane, a writer, editor, and researcher of historical collections, graduated from Western Business College. She worked in the healthcare field as a medical assistant and has continued her education in this field. She also coaches on health and fitness.

Karen worked as a project-control manager for an aerospace contractor in San Diego for almost thirty years and now resides in Washington State with her husband. She is an award-winning author, garnering a WILLA, two Will Roger Medallions, and the San Diego Book Award. She writes under her pen name, **KB Taylor**. Her books can be viewed on her website: ***kb-taylor.com.***

KAREN, DOUG, AND DIANE TAYLOR
1985

**MOM AND DAD
DOUG, DIANE AND KAREN
Doug's Twelfth birthday
(Sixth grade)**

**DOUG 1969
High School Graduate**

**KAREN AND DIANE
Seventh and Fifth Grade**

AUTHORS' EARLY GRAYS-HARBOR FAMILY HISTORY

GREAT-GRANDFATHER Fred Cline, arrived to Hoquiam in 1888. During his life, he was the portlight tender for the Westport channel, crew member on the bar tug *Printer,* boilerman on the tugboat *Traveler,* a sea captain, a boatbuilder, inventor, and builder of pile-driven fish traps at the mouth of the Humptulips River. He built nine sea-faring boats, five of them steam-powered. His largest was the *Irene* at sixty-feet.

Great-grandmother, Lizzie Snyder, arrived in 1884. She ran a Hoquiam boardinghouse and later became a Sanipractic (Naturopathic) physician in Hoquiam for twenty-eight years. She was Lester Hanson's mother.

Great-uncles Charles and Marion Veysey (pronounced Vee-Cee) arrived to Montesano in 1892, where they opened their first of six mercantile stores[gg] in Grays Harbor County. Great-grandfather Leon Veysey, became manager of the Hoquiam store in 1902, and by 1908, was the president of the Veysey Bros. Company. Leon and Charles Veysey's biographies were published in the *Washington, West of the Cascades* book, Vol. 3, by Author Herbert Hunt, 1917, Page 398-399. In 1906, Charles Veysey ran as the Republican candidate for the Washington State Senate. He lost, but his son Victor went on to be a United States Congressman, representing California, and was the Assistant Secretary of the Army under President Ford.

Great-grandparents, Nettie Connell, teacher and assistant principal at McKinley, and Mastin Taylor, business owner[hh] and Hoquiam councilman, arrived to Hoquiam in 1896 and Mastin in 1898. Based on the 1900 United States Census, Agnes Connell, age eighteen, was living with Nettie and Mastin at their Ninth Street home and was attending school. Nettie would have been her teacher. Six years later, Agnes married Harry Hubble, Captain of Hubble Tugboats. Agnes' marriage certificate listed "sales lady" as her occupation. She along with her sisters, Carrie and Ruth, were working in Mastin and Nettie's store, the Economy Company, also referred to as the Temple of Economy, and advertised as the *working man's store.*

[gg] Veysey six stores: Aberdeen, Hoquiam, Elma, and three in Montesano. Thirty-five years.

[hh] Mastin Taylor owned two Hoquiam businesses: the Temple of Economy and Taylor Fruit and Produce on Levee Street.

(LtoR:) 1899, Nettie Connell Taylor (Asst. Principal/Teacher) with her **sister Agnes Connell** in front of the Hoquiam Economy Company store.

Harry Hubble named above tugboat "AGNES"
(Courtesy of the Polson Museum, Hoquiam, Wash. 2002.043.0017)

1931, Nettie "Connell" Taylor with brother **RAY CONNELL** and his four children (LtoR): Margaret holding baby Ray, **DOROTHYE** and AnnaRae

REFERENCES

> 40
>
> Hoquiam March 28th 1891.
>
> Regular meeting Board Trustees of School district No. 28.
>
> Members present. Geo H Emerson J A Karr and Seth Warren.
>
> Records of previous meeting read and approved. The Secretary reported the payment of Sundry Bills. On motion action of Secretary was approved.
>
> Motion by J A Karr. That it is the sense of this Board. that a building site for School building be secured in Karr's River addition and one in vicinity of 5th and L Streets Hoquiam. (motion carried)
>
> On motion the present session of Schools shall terminate on May 22d 1891. so ordered.
>
> Motion by Warren that School clerk be instructed to have school loh graded sufficient for Comfort. (carried).
>
> Motion by J A Karr that the course of study presented by Mr Adams principal be adopted and spread upon the records (carried)

1891 HOQUIAM SCHOOL BOARD NOTES
(Courtesy of Larry R. Jones' collection)

Hoquiam Graded School.
Course of Study
Primary Department.

Principal Clark

Reading. Chart and First Reader, completed with drill in reading script characters.

Numbers. Teach numbers from <u>one</u> to <u>ten</u>. Follow the course outlined in Parker's Talks on Teaching, chapters XVI & XVII. (Wentworth's primary in the hands of Teacher.)

Language. Teach the correct use of language by constantly correcting common errors. Give special attention to terminal marks and capitals.

Writing. Use only pencils and crayons. Teach correct forms of small letters and capitals.

Spelling. Teach both oral and written from reading lessons. Attention to sounds of letters.

Hygiene. Occasional short lectures on laws of health. Special attention to correct position in sitting and standing.

Drawing. Daily drill in simple exercises (Hull's Exercises in the hands of teacher.

1891 HOQUIAM GRADED SCHOOL "COURSE OF STUDY"
(Courtesy of Larry R. Jones' collection)

Secondary Department
Second Grade.

Reading — Second Reader – completed

Numbers — Teach numbers from ten to twenty, reading and writing of numbers to twenty in Arabic and Roman characters. and the signs of equality, plus, minus, of multiplication and division. Teachers will adopt the plan outlined in chapters XV, XVI, and XVII, Parker's Talks on Teaching. (Wentworth's Primary Arith. in hands of teacher.)

Writing — Copy book No. 1. in fall term and No. 2. during Spring term.

Spelling — Oral and written from reader. Phonetic drill.

Geography — Develop the idea of right and left. Teach cardinal and semi-cardinal points. Hold conversational lessons about trees, animals, plants, valleys, rivers etc.

Language — Hold frequent conversational lessons. Lead pupils to form sentences involving the use of words found in the Second reader. Develope the ideas of telling and asking sentences. Teach correct use of *a* and *an*. Insist upon complete sentences in answer to questions.

1891 HOQUIAM GRADED SCHOOL "COURSE OF STUDY"
(Courtesy of Larry R. Jones' collection)

Secondary Department
Third Grade

Fall Term — 16 weeks.

- **Reading** — Third Reader, throughout the year
- **Arithmetic** — Wentworth's primary, review the work done in the first and second Grades. Complete Chapter V (Book in the hands of pupils
- **Language** — Hyde's First Book, Part I
- **Spelling** — Oral and written words from the Third Reader. Have frequent exercises in Phonetic spelling. Thorough drill in diacritical marks throughout the year.
- **Writing** — Complete Grammar Grade. No 3.
- **Geography** — Teach names of principal divisions of land and water.

Spring Term — 20 weeks.

- **Reading** — Continue work of Fall term.
- **Spelling** — Words from Third Reader and first 60 lessons in Modern Speller.
- **Arithmetic** — Wentworth's primary Chapter VI
- **Hygiene** — Pathfinder No 1 in hands of Teacher.
- **Language** — Hyde's First Book completed
- **Writing** — Complete Grammar Grade. No 4.
- **Geography** — Drill on maps of continents. Map drawing.

1891 HOQUIAM GRADED SCHOOL "COURSE OF STUDY"
(Courtesy of Larry R. Jones' collection)

44

Intermediate Department
Fourth Grade.
Fall Term, 16 weeks

Reading. Third Reader completed with supplementary reading if possible. Drill on diacritical marks throughout the year.
Spelling Modern speller. pages 25 to 40, inclusive.
Arithmetic Wentworth's primary reviewed and completed.
Geography Harper's introductory. (Book not yet at hand.)
Writing Complete Grammarian Grade No 5.
Language Oral lessons. Parts of Speech taught.

Spring Term 20 weeks.

Reading Fourth Reader begun.
Spelling Modern Speller. Pages 41 to 62, inclusive.
Arithmetic Wentworth's Grammar School, chapters I, II, III.
Geography Harper's introductory, completed.
Writing Complete Grammarian Grade No 6.
Language Complete first four chapters in Meeks first lessons in English.

1891 HOQUIAM GRADED SCHOOL "COURSE OF STUDY"
(Courtesy of Larry R. Jones' collection)

Intermediate Department
Fifth Grade.
Fall term — 16 weeks.

Reading	Fourth Reader continued, Drill in use of diacritical marks. Phonetic spelling &c throughout the year
Spelling	Modern Speller, pages 63 to 82 inclusive
History	Eggleston's First Book completed.
Grammar	Welsh's. First lessons Chapter V. preceded by a breif review of the essential points in chapters I, II, III, & IV
Arithmetic	Wentworth's Grammar School, chapters IV & V
Hygiene	Pathfinder No 2. Completed.
Writing	Gramman Grade No 7. Completed.

Spring Term — 20 weeks.

Reading	Fourth Reader completed with supplementary reading
Spelling	Modern Speller pages 83 to 105 inclusive
Grammar	Welsh's first lessons completed.
Arithmetic	Wentworth's Grammar School. Chapters VI & VII
Geography	Harpers School. First 32 & last 17 pages.
Civics	Griffin's For young Americans completed
Writing	Gramman Grade No 8. Completed.

1891 HOQUIAM GRADED SCHOOL "COURSE OF STUDY"
(Courtesy of Larry R. Jones' collection)

Principal's Department
Sixth Grade

Fall Term — 16 weeks

Reading	Franklin Fifth reader begun.
Spelling	Modern Speller Pages 106 to 125 inclusive
History	Eggleston's to Chapter XXVII
Arithmetic	Wentworth's Grammar School, Chapter VIII
Ment. Arith	Brook's Normal Mental First two sections.
Geography	Harpers. School. Pages 33 to 63 inclusive
Writing	Principles of Spencerian System taught general practice and writing of notes, drafts, receipts bills, letters etc.

Spring Term 20 weeks

Reading	Fifth Reader continued with supplementary reading
Spelling	Modern Speller. pages 126 to 147 inclusive
History	Eggleston's U.S. Chapter XXVII – LXI inclusive
Grammar	Welch's, first 15 chapters
Arithmetic	Wentworth's Grammar School. Chapter IX & X
Ment. Arith	Brooks Normal. Sections III & IV
Geography	Harpers School pages 64 – 99 inclusive

1891 HOQUIAM GRADED SCHOOL "COURSE OF STUDY"
(Courtesy of Larry R. Jones' collection)

(Authors' collection)
1930 Newspaper saved by Taylor family

Excerpt:
Pennies contributed by school children in **Hoquiam** and other American communities made possible the reconditioning of the historic frigate, pictured here as it was set afloat at the Charleston, Mass. Navy yard after being under construction for three years.

1933 HOQUIAM HIGH SCHOOL BAND
At "Old Ironsides" Port Dock
(Courtesy of the Polson Museum, Hoquiam, Wash.
2006.012.0002)

During the 1812 battle, a British sailor hollered, "Huzza," her sides are made of iron!" She was later christened "Old Ironsides."

REFERENCES

HOQUIAM HIGH SCHOOL Graduating Classes

Year	Count	Year	Count	Year	Count	Year	Count
1891	2	1920	36	1949	120	1979	191
1892	4	1921	39	1950	114	1980	190
1893	4	1922	55	1951	102	1981	177
1894	8	1923	68	1952	108	1982	163
1895	5	1924	74	1953	108	1983	153
1896	7	1925	80	1954	121	1984	135
1897	9	1926	100	1955	149	1985	140
1898	5	1927	79	1956	127	1986	194
1899	5	1928	98	1957	145	1987	123
1900	8	1929	98	1958	130	1988	177
1901	5	1930	132	1959	151	1989	153
1902	6	1931	122	1960	169	1990	105
1903	4	1932	185	1961	165	1991	111
1904	4	1933	156	1962	144	1992	114
1905	0	1934	128	1963	140	1993	143
1906	4	1935	128	1964	153	1994	115
1907	7	1936	156	1965	211	1995	132
1908	7	1937	147	1966	196	1996	121
1909	11	1938	153	1967	213	1997	135
1910	18	1939	160	1968	248	1998	140
1911	9	1940	159	1969	218	1999	119
1912	13	1941	168	1970	199	2000	121
1913	23	1942	151	1971	204	2001	117
1914	28	1943	143	1972	192	2002	116
1915	29	1944	88	1973	190	2003	122
1916	27	1945	89	1974	281	2004	120
1917	38	1946	127	1975	212	2005	120
1918	39	1947	112	1976	176	2006	112
1919	35	1948	117	1977	183	2007	110
				1978	179		

HOQUIAM HIGH SCHOOL "GRADUATING CLASS HEADCOUNT"
(Courtesy of Larry R. Jones' collection)

Note the decrease during WWII (1944 and 1945)

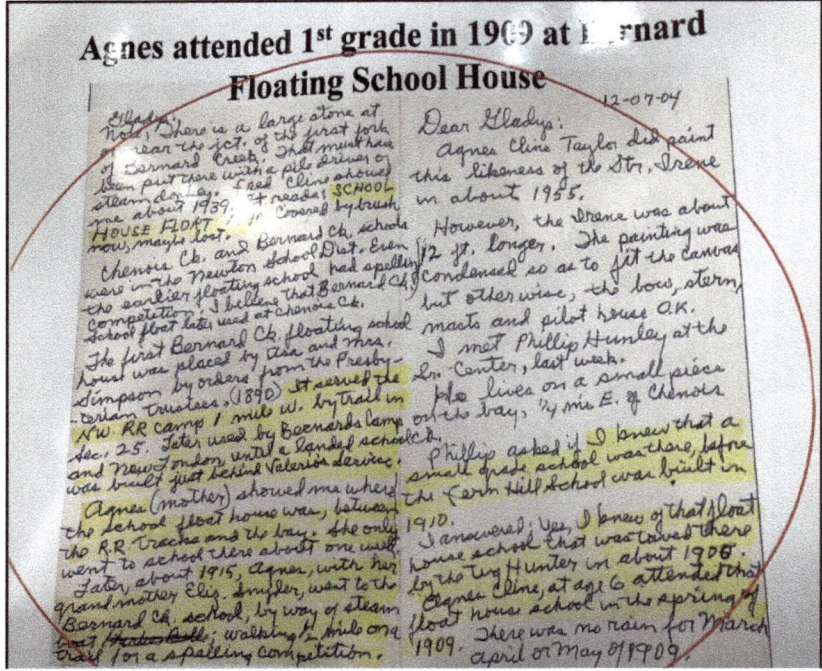

BERNARD FLOATING SCHOOL HOUSE (1909)
(Authors' collection)

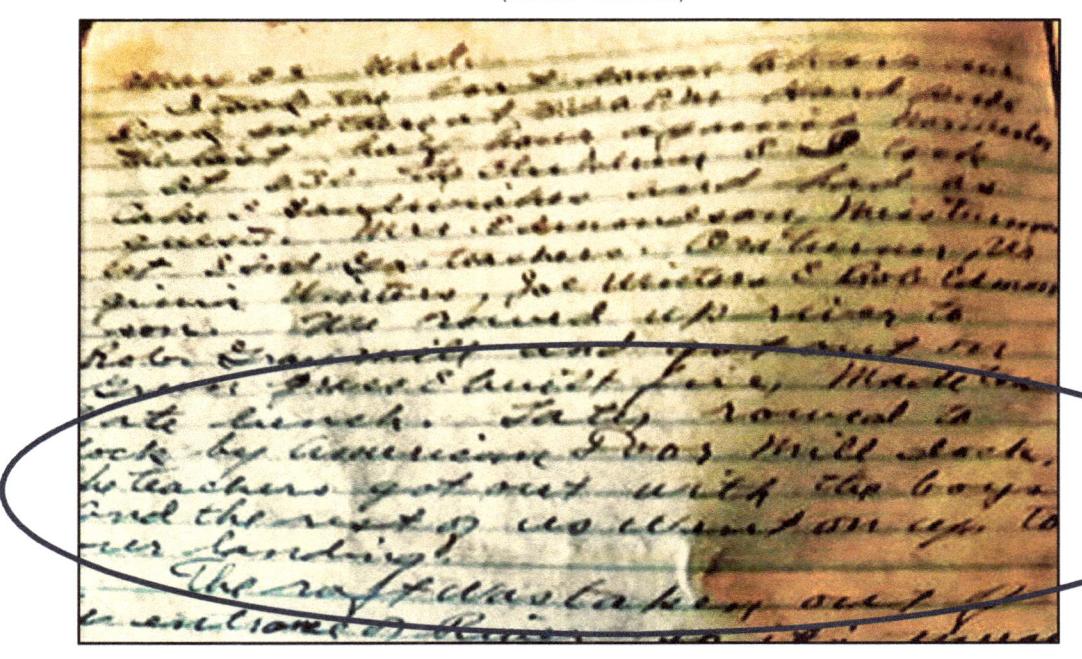

SKOOKUM LOG (1934) SCHOOL BOAT
School teachers aboard
Agnes Taylor May 23, 1934
(Authors' collection)

REFERENCES

**1940 HOQUIAM HIGH SCHOOL GRADUATE
GLADYS MAY**
Viorene "Gladys" Muhlhauser (née May)
(Authors' cousin)

Gladys' high school days were during the 1930 Depression years, following the 1929 stock-market crash. She attended Emerson Grade School, Hoquiam Junior High, and graduated from Hoquiam High School in 1940. Many of her artifacts pieced this book together.

Great-aunt Viorene Cline (circled)
First grade 1911
McKinley School classroom
(Authors' collection)

NOTES

INTRODUCTION
1. *A Brief Historical Sketch of Grays Harbor, Washington*, Willam D. Welsh of Rayonier Incorp, Pg 13
2. *Washington, West of the Cascades*, Volume II,1917, Herbert Hunt, Pg 86; Polson Museum, Hoquiam Sash and Door Company writeup, 2001.018.0102.
3. *A Brief Historical Sketch of Grays Harbor, Washington*, Willam D. Welsh of Rayonier Incorp, Pg 13
4. Ibid
5. *Washington, West of the Cascades*, Volume II,1917, Herbert Hunt, Pg 87
6. Ibid, Pg 89
7. *Washington State Historical Society*, James A. Karr & Abbie Walker; *Washington, West of the Cascades*, Volume II,1917, Herbert Hunt, Pg 88, 89
8. *Washington, West of the Cascades*, Volume II,1917, Herbert Hunt, Pg 87
9. Ibid, Pg 87
10. Ibid, Pg 88
11. Ibid, Pg 80
12. NW 979.7, U.S. Works Progress Administration, Washington State. *Told by the Pioneers*. Vol. 3, Pg 191
13. *Washington, West of the Cascades*, Volume II,1917, Herbert Hunt, Pg 89
14. Ibid, Pg 90 (James A. Karr)
15. *A Brief Historical Sketch of Grays Harbor, Washington*, Willam D. Welsh of Rayonier Incorp, Pg13
16. *The River Pioneers, Early Days on Grays Harbor*, Edwin Van Syckle, pg. 252
17. *A Brief Historical Sketch of Grays Harbor, Washington*, Willam D. Welsh of Rayonier Incorp, Pg 13
18. *The River Pioneers, Early Days on Grays Harbor*, Edwin Van Syckle, pg. 253
19. Ibid, pg. 255
20. Ibid, pg. 259
21. *A Brief Historical Sketch of Grays Harbor, Washington*, Willam D. Welsh of Rayonier Incorp, Pgs 12-13
22. *The River Pioneers, Early Days on Grays Harbor*, Edwin Van Syckle, Pg 372
23. *They Tried to Cut it All*, Edwin Van Syckle, Pgs 12-13
24. *Grays Harbor*, 1885-1913, Robsert A. Weinstein, Pgs17-18
25. *City of Hoquiam is incorporated on May 21, 1890* by Aaron Goings, posted 9/3/2008, HistoryLink.org Essay8722, Pg 3
26. Ibid, Pg 1

CHAPTER 1– FIRST SCHOOLS
1. *The River Pioneers, Early Days on Grays Harbor*, Edwin Van Syckle, pg. 372, Hoquiam School 1874: James A. Karr and Edward Campbell 1880 United States census provides children's ages.
2. NW 979.7, U.S. Works Progress Administration, Washington State. *Told by the Pioneers*. Vol. 3, Pg 191; *The River Pioneers, Early Days on Grays Harbor*, Edwin Van Syckle, pg. 372: James A. Karr and Edward Campbell 1880 United States census.
3. 1906 *Hoquiam High yearbook reaches way back*, Ade Fredericksen, Daily World, June 12, 1988.
4. *The River Pioneers, Early Days on Grays Harbor*, Edwin Van Syckle Pg 372.
5. Ibid, Pg 373.
6. Ibid, Pg 372.

7. *School Days' 1900* by Clara Knack Dooley, Pgs 39-40. *The River Pioneers, Early Days on Grays Harbor*, Edwin Van Syckle, pg. 372, Stevens School built in 1882 and enlarged somewhat in 1889.
8. 1906 Hesperian yearbook
9. *Hoquiam High School 100 Years of Grizzly Pride!* 1891-1991 booklet, Pg 2
10. *School Days' 1900* by Clara Knack Dooley, Pg 42
11. Ibid, Pg 15
12. Ibid, Pg 3, Pg 34
13. Ibid, Pg 4-5
14. *Hoquiam High School 100 Years of Grizzly Pride!* 1891-1991 booklet, Pg 2; *School Days' 1900*, Clara Knack Dooley, Pg 10
15. 1906 Hesperian yearbook
16. *School Days' 1900* by Clara Knack Dooley, Pg 40
17. Ibid, Pg 28
18. Ibid, Pg 71
19. Ibid, Pg 55
20. *Hoquiam Sawyer* (formerly Gant's Sawyer), front page, March 26, 1904, Pg 1 and 2
21. Ibid
22. *School Days' 1900*, Clara Knack Dooley, Pg 56-57

CHAPTER 2—TEACHERS
1. *The River Pioneers, Early Days on Grays Harbor*, Edwin Van Syckle, pg. 372
2. NW 979.7, U.S. Works Progress Administration, Washington State. *Told by the Pioneers*. Vol. 3, Pg 191.
3. *The River Pioneers, Early Days on Grays Harbor*, Edwin Van Syckle, pg. 259
4. Polson Museum 2001.031.0003 description, Julius Andrews, first teacher; 1880/1890 United States Census.
5. Ibid, Pg 372.

CHAPTER 3—OTHER SCHOOLS
1. Per Lee Thomasson's research.
2. Paul B. Taylor postcard to Gladys M. dated 12/07/2004
3. Increased immigration placed new demands on public schools, pg 5, **www.cep-dc-org,**

CHAPTER 5—A NEW DECADE
1. *The Hoquiam Alumnus* booklet, July 2, 1913, Pg 2
2. Ibid, Pg 12
3. *Hoquiam High School 100 Years of Grizzly Pride!* 1891-1991 booklet, Year 1913, Pg 7
4. Larry Jones worked with Ray Thurber at Lincoln Elementary in 1957.
5. Ibid, Pg 8
6. Polson Museum, Harbor History Highlight, "Grippe Hits Home: The 1918 Influenza Pandemic on Grays Harbor," John Larson, Museum Director, July 2020.
7. *Hoquiam High School 100 Years of Grizzly Pride!* 1891-1991 booklet, Year 1913, Pg 8

CHAPTER 6—THE 1920S
1. 1928 *Hesperian*, The Commerce Department.
2. 1930 Hesperian, Freshman notes.

CHAPTER 7—THE GREAT DEPRESSION YEARS
1. *The History of Kindergarten: From Germany to the United States* by Christina More Muelle, Florida International University, USA, Pg 87 – 92.
2. *Growing Up in Hoquiam, My First Eighteen Years, 1930-1948,* by Janice Warford Fisher, Kindergarten, Pg 16-17

NOTES

3 Ibid, Pg 19
4 *Flooding of 1933 was worst,* Ade Fredericksen, Daily World,
5 1931 *Hesperian,* Yell Leaders.
6 *Hoquiam High School 100 Years of Grizzly Pride!* 1891-1991 booklet, Year 1913, Pg 13
7 The Aberdeen Daily World, September 17, 1965, Pg 6., *Hoquiam Enjoyed Athletic Heyday During the Thirties,* by Ray Ryan

CHAPTER 8—WWII AND AFTER

1 *Growing Up in Hoquiam, My First Eighteen Years, 1930-1948,* by Janice Warford Fisher, Pg 56
2 Ibid, Pg 54
3 Ibid, Pg 55-56
4 HistoryLink.org Essay 10649: *Crowd smashes store windows and lights in Seattle blackout riots on December 8, 1949.* Duane Colt Denfeld, Ph.D. 12/02/2013.
5 *Growing Up in Hoquiam, My First Eighteen Years, 1930-1948,* by Janice Warford Fisher, Pg 53
6 *Hoquiam High School 100 Years of Grizzly Pride!* 1891-1991 booklet, Year 1913, Pg 16
7 *Growing Up in Hoquiam, My First Eighteen Years, 1930-1948,* by Janice Warford Fisher, Pg 42

CHAPTER 10—CENTRAL No. 3

1 The Aberdeen Daily World, March 4, 1954, *Central School Dedication Tonight*

CHAPTER 12—EMERSON ELEMENTARY

1 First-hand knowledge from Larry R. Jones, a personal friend of Miss Rosenberg.

CHAPTER 13—LINCOLN ELEMENTARY SCHOOL

1 Boat Log, Pg 167
2 *The Age of Enrollment and Space.* Lincoln School. Larry Jones Collection.

CHAPTER 14—WASHINGTON SCHOOL

1 *Growing Up in Hoquiam, My First Eighteen Years, 1930-1948,* by Janice Warford Fisher, Pg 21
2 Ibid, Pg 25
3 Ibid, Pg 24-28.
4 Ibid, Pg 27-28
5 Ibid, Pg 9

CHAPTER 16—SCHOOL RELATED ACTIVITIES

1 *Growing Up in Hoquiam, My First Eighteen Years, 1930-1948,* by Janice Warford Fisher, Pg 69-70
2 Grays Harbor *Washingtonian,* Friday Morning, August 4, 1939, Pg 4 and 5, Titled: *Spectacle will be Shown at Stadium.*

CHAPTER 17—HOQUIAM PUBLIC LIBRARY

1 Hoquiam Timberland Library, History Highlights pamphlet, 1911 to 2011.
2 Ibid

CHAPTER 18—THE EVOLUTION OF HOQUIAM'S SCHOOLS, DISTRICT 28

1 *School Days' 1900* by Clara Knack Dooley.
2 The Aberdeen Daily World, *Central Elementary* 1954.

CHAPTER 19—CENTRAL 1,2,3

1 The Aberdeen Daily World, *Central Elementary* 1954.

(Update 12/29/24)

www.ingramcontent.com/pod-product-compliance
Lightning Source LLC
LaVergne TN
LVHW070522070526
838199LV00072B/6674